Great Documents
in U.S. History

EARLY SETTLEMENT TO RECONSTRUCTION (1620–1870)

Volume I

Richard Kollen

J. WESTON
WALCH
PUBLISHER

JWW131   v1.01

ISBN 978-0-8251-5905-3

Copyright © 2006

J. Weston Walch, Publisher

P.O. Box 802 I Culver City, CA 90232

www.socialstudies.com/walch

Printed in the United States of America

Contents

To the Teacher

The material in this volume is presented to allow maximum teacher flexibility in how it is used in the classroom.

Each document and exercise can be used in a variety of ways. Here are three.

1. Have students work independently on the questions, some or all, to be discussed as a class later.

2. Have students work in small groups on the questions. The groups can do the following:

   • Work on all of them together.
   • Divide the questions among members to work on independently. Members can then explain their answers to their group.

3. As a teacher-directed activity, do the exercises as a whole group.

The exercises that follow the documents are divided into question sets by type.

Comprehension Questions. The comprehension questions simply require a literal understanding of the documents.

Critical Thinking. The "Critical Thinking" question set requires students to go beyond the document text. Some questions call for an assessment of the information's reliability. Many students are likely to take as fact anything written by a firsthand source. Teachers may need to lead students to evaluate sources. As explained in the student introductory section, certain factors influence the message in a primary source. Among these are author, source, and audience.

Making Connections. Students should have had exposure to the historical issues that each document addresses before reading the documents. Nonetheless, an introduction providing background precedes each document. Teachers may decide not to have students read this and instead use it themselves to teach the documents. It should be understood that the "Making Connections" question sets often rely on outside information, both regarding events surrounding the source and previous sources. Context is critical to students creating meaning out of the documents.

Relating the Past to Our Lives. This question set asks students to connect the document to their lives or to the modern United States. It is designed for students to see the relevance of history today.

Essay Questions. These call for an extended answer. This may be in the form of a written essay or perhaps in large- or small-group discussion.

Note: Some of the documents are shortened versions. Missing portions are designated by ellipses (. . .). In most documents, the original spelling has been preserved, except where archaic spellings might be difficult for students.

To the Student

Reading and Interpreting Primary Source Documents

Primary sources are the raw material of history. They include but are not limited to the following:

letters	report cards	laws
advertisements	oral histories	photographs
diaries	maps	objects
bills	autobiographies	programs
speeches	drawings	

They are documents and objects left by people who participated in or witnessed events. Historians interpret this evidence to write secondary sources—books, such as your textbook. The key word here is *interpret*. With most records, there is room for disagreement on their meanings.

Interpreting primary sources, then, is as basic to the historian's work as performing experiments is to the scientist. It is how they reach conclusions about what they are studying. As history students, you need to learn to interpret primary sources as part of your study. What follows are hints for getting the most out of reading the primary sources included in this book.

1. Identifying the Document

What type of document is it? What is its purpose? Who is the audience?

Answering the first question helps to answer the second two. For example, a friendly letter usually has a limited audience due to its purpose. A speech, however, will have a much broader audience. This matters. Some ideas a person might disclose in a private letter he or she would not include in a public speech. Think about what you would write in a letter to your closest friend about a teacher. Compare that with what you might say about the teacher in a speech at a school assembly. People make speeches to persuade or inform. The speaker understands that the audience will be mixed and that the message needs to be tailored to this. A letter to a friend has a different purpose and audience. Therefore, it contains different information.

2. Placing the Document in Its Context

When was the document created? What was happening in the country at this time?

Knowing about the circumstances that surround the primary source's creation is important. This places the document in its context. It helps the historian to grasp its full meaning.

For example, a student writes an editorial in the school newspaper calling for more diversity in faculty hiring. Twenty years later someone researching a history of the school reads the editorial. The researcher would want to know about the circumstances surrounding the editorial.

- Did the editorial represent a large number of students with a similar opinion, or was the author a lone voice?
- What was the racial makeup of the staff at the time?
- What was the racial makeup of the student body?

Answers to these and other questions would help the historian understand the document by placing it in context.

Who created the document? What do you know about that person? What was his or her role in the events?

Answering these questions furthers the historian's understanding of the context. Imagine reading excerpts from a diary written by your brother or sister ten years earlier. Your knowledge of the circumstances of his or her life at the time—about friends, home, interests, opinions, problems, and so forth—would make the diary much more understandable. Now imagine someone reading it who never knew your brother or sister or anything about his or her life. That person's understanding would be seriously weakened— unless he or she did some research. You can place the diary in its proper context. The other reader cannot.

Context is provided before each document in this book in the sections titled "Historical Context" and "Importance." You may want to read this material first. What you learn in history class about the time period will add to your knowledge of the document's circumstances. It is likely your teacher will assign the documents in this book when you study the time in which they were created.

3. Reading and Understanding the Document
What are the key words in the source and what do they mean?

When reading documents, the language can be difficult. This can be especially true when documents were written a long time ago. Today, we value clear, direct language. This was not necessarily true in the past. It is important when you read the documents in this book to understand the meanings of the words used in the documents. Keep each document's vocabulary list with definitions close by for reference.

What is the message? What point is the author trying to make? What evidence does the author give to support the point?

All documents have a main idea or message. It could be helpful to jot down what you believe is the main idea after reading a document. Listing the evidence used to support the main idea will also help your understanding.

4. Evaluating the Document

How reliable is the document? Is the information supported by other evidence?

Historians must take this task very seriously because they will read many documents surrounding an event. The information provided by these documents may differ slightly. In some cases, the documents might contradict one another. This leaves the historian to make a judgment about what to believe. One way to make the judgment is to check for other sources that support it. Your textbook or other primary sources can help in determining whether other information supports the facts stated in a document.

In what ways might the information be biased?

All documents are biased to some degree. The creator always has a point of view on an issue or event. The information the author wants his or her audience to know becomes the message. Certain facts could be left out or slanted in a particular way. This might be done on purpose. For example, when you make an argument, are you likely to include the evidence that hurts your position?

But bias may not be conscious. For example, consider a loud argument between two students in a school hallway. This may be reported differently by observers depending on the following:

- their location in the hallway

- their relationship with one of the students involved

- to whom they are reporting the event

- how soon after the event it is reported

The historian takes nothing at face value. Instead, she or he weighs the factors of creator, purpose, audience, and context to determine the reliability of the document.

Consider these ideas when reading the documents in this volume. Approach them as a historian just as you perform experiments as a scientist in chemistry class.

The Mayflower Compact

Document: The Mayflower Compact (1620)

Historical Context

The situation called for action. The *Mayflower*, a British ship, had carried 102 passengers across the Atlantic Ocean. They had traveled 3,000 miles only to land north of their destination. They had hoped to begin a colony at the mouth of the Hudson River, the site of today's New York City. This would have placed the colony within the geographic boundaries the king outlined in the Virginia Company of Plymouth's charter. This group of businessmen invested money to start the colony. In return they hoped to profit from the products of the New World. The company's charter outlined how the settlement would be governed. But the *Mayflower*'s passengers had drifted outside the charter's boundaries. Now they were off the tip of Cape Cod on November 9, 1620, with no laws to govern them. The passenger list showed that the colonists needed to create a government.

- About one third was a group later called Pilgrims, the organizers of the colony. They had separated from the Church of England over religious differences. The Pilgrims had lived for a time in Holland. Now they hoped to make a new start.
- The rest of the passengers were skilled workers and servants who sought a new life. They were members of the Church of England. The Pilgrims called them "Strangers."

Pilgrim William Bradford wrote about what happened. As the *Mayflower* neared shore, its passengers realized they were outside of the area covered by the charter. Arguments began among the "Strangers" and Pilgrims. Clearly, a temporary government was needed. One of the Pilgrims drew up an agreement, or compact. It was later called the Mayflower Compact because passengers signed it while still on board the *Mayflower*. It was based on the way the Pilgrims governed their church. Every male head of household and male bachelor, as well as three male servants, signed the compact on November 11, 1620. The signers pledged to obey any laws agreed to by the majority.

Later, the ship's passengers settled in a more sheltered harbor in today's Massachusetts for their permanent colony. Called Plymouth, it was the first New England colony. In the first couple of years about one half of the original colonists died of starvation and disease, even with the help of the Indians. But the colony survived, and its people worked together.

Importance

It was not until after the American Revolution that the Mayflower Compact received much attention. At this time the new nation began looking back to the roots of its self-government. Today, the compact is often viewed as the first example of American democracy, a social contract. But it is also understood that the idea came from the practical need for unity to survive in the wilderness.

The Mayflower Compact (1620)

In the name of God Amen. We, whose names are underwritten, the loyal subjects of our dread sovereign Lord King James by the grace of God, of Great Britain, France, and Ireland king, defender of the Faith, etc.

Having undertaken, for the glory of God, and advancement of the Christian faith and honour of our king and country, a voyage to plant the first colony in the northern parts of Virginia. Do by these presents solemnly and mutually in the presence of God, and one of another, covenant and combine our selves together into a civil body politic; for our better ordering, and preservation and furtherance of the ends aforesaid; and by virtue hereof to enact, constitute, and frame such just and equal laws, ordinances, acts, constitutions and offices, from time to time, as shall be thought most meet and convenient for the general good of the Colony: unto which we promise all due submission and obedience. In witness whereof we have hereunder subscribed our names at Cape Cod, the 11 of November, in the year of the reign of our sovereign Lord King James of England, France, and Ireland the eighteenth and of Scotland the fifty-fourth. Anno Dom. 1620.

John Carver	Richard Warren	Thomas Williams
William Bradford	John Howland	Gilbert Winslow
Edward Winslow	Steven Hopkins	Edmond Margeson
William Brewster	Edward Tilly	Peter Brown
Isaac Allerton	John Tilly	Richard Bitteridge
Miles Standish	Francis Cook	Richard Clark
John Alden	Thomas Rogers	Richard Gardiner
Samuel Fuller	Thomas Tinker	John Allerton
Christopher Martin	John Rigdale	Thomas English
William Mullins	Edward Fuller	Edward Doten
William White	John Turner	Edward Liester
James Chilton	Francis Eaton	John Goodman
John Craxton	Moses Fletcher	George Soule
John Billington	Digery Priest	

Vocabulary

dread—causing great fear

sovereign—ruler, king

grace—undeserved help from God

undertaken—having taken upon oneself

solemnly—seriously

mutually—acting together in common

covenant—pledge

civil body politic—the people organized as a nation considered as a group

furtherance—the act of advancing

aforesaid—previously mentioned

by virtue (of)—by reason (of)

hereof—of this

ordinances—commands by an authority

submission—the act of giving in to the power of another

whereof—of what

subscribed—signed one's name

reign—period during which a king rules

Anno Dom.—short for *Anno Domini,* "in the year of our Lord" (after the birth of Christ); usually written A.D.

Comprehension Questions

1. According to the Mayflower Compact, what was the purpose of the voyage?

2. Where were the voyagers intending to land? Where did they end up?

3. What is the reason the signers combine into "a civil body politic"?

4. What do the signers promise?

5. When was the compact signed?

6. What was the gender of the signers?

Critical Thinking

1. Why do you think the Mayflower Compact begins as it does?

2. What is the document's main idea?

3. Who is the document's audience?

4. What is the most important idea in the document?

5. What might have happened if the *Mayflower*'s passengers had not created this agreement?

6. Why has the Mayflower Compact gained such importance in our nation's history?

Making Connections

1. Is the Mayflower Compact a democratic document? Explain.

2. Why did people aboard the *Mayflower* believe it was necessary for the men to agree to the compact, but not the women?

3. Why didn't the settlers of the earlier British colony of Jamestown create a similar document?

4. What other groups came to the United States for religious freedom?

5. How does the Mayflower Compact compare in importance with other important documents such as the Declaration of Independence and the U.S. Constitution? Which do you think the compact is more like? Explain.

Relating the Past to Our Lives

1. Imagine being shipwrecked on a deserted island. How might something like the Mayflower Compact help your group survive?

2. What groups do you belong to that are governed by the group's members?

3. The Virginia Company of Plymouth hoped to make a profit on its investment in the colony. Have you ever invested money for a later profit? If so, in what? Did you in fact make a profit?

Essay Questions

1. Which laws do you think the colonists will create first? Why?

2. Why do you think this document was identified later as significant?

3. How do you think the two groups in the new colony got along? What were the dividing factors? What were the unifying factors? How does creating the compact further unity?

Common Sense

Document: Thomas Paine, *Common Sense* (1776)

Historical Context

Occasionally a book is published that shifts public opinion concerning an important event. *Common Sense* by Thomas Paine was such a book. Many Patriots argued that Britain should stop its unfair taxation. Paine went further. He wrote that common sense determined that nothing less than full independence should be the American colonies' goal. Paine's book was published during the colonies' crisis with Britain. Many historians believe that this book shaped public support for independence.

The first edition of *Common Sense* was published in January 1776. This was after the war had begun but before many Americans were willing to take the final step of separation from their mother country. A second larger edition came out a month later. *Common Sense* sold 120,000 copies in the first three months. In a country of 1.5 million people, 500,000 copies were sold by the end of the year. It had become America's first best seller.

The Second Continental Congress continued its meeting in Philadelphia in 1776. It contained representatives whose colonies had denied permission for them to vote for independence. Did *Common Sense* alone change public opinion? Events rarely have a single cause. But historians credit *Common Sense* with having the single greatest influence on public opinion. Paine had a way of expressing the ideals of the Revolution in an understandable manner. Soon Patriot conventions were being held throughout the colonies urging independence. In July independence was declared.

Thomas Paine, son of a corset maker, met Benjamin Franklin in London. Following Franklin's advice, Paine came to the American colonies in 1774. Once in the colonies, Paine wrote for *Pennsylvania Magazine*. After writing *Common Sense* he joined the Continental Army in 1776. In 1776 and 1777, he published *The Crisis,* designed to inspire support for the war among average American colonists. After the war he traveled to Europe. He continued his revolutionary work there by supporting the French Revolution.

Importance

Paine understood the American Revolution's importance to the world. No colonial people had won their independence before. Paine wrote that independence was America's natural right. Not only did he argue for independence, but also he urged that a republican government be formed. This, Paine believed, could instruct the world. In *Common Sense* Paine uses the technique of first raising the opposition's argument, then explaining why it is wrong. He also makes comparisons everyone can understand, such as the mother-child relationship compared with the colonial relationship. Although logical, Paine's language can be emotional also.

5

Thomas Paine, *Common Sense*, 1776

I have heard it asserted by some, that as America has flourished under her former connection with Great Britain, the same connection is necessary towards her future happiness, and will always have the same effect. Nothing can be more fallacious than this kind of argument. We may as well assert that because a child has thrived upon milk, that it is never to have meat, or that the first twenty years of our lives is to become a precedent for the next twenty. But even this is admitting more than is true; for I answer roundly, that America would have flourished as much, and probably much more, had no European power taken any notice of her. The commerce by which she hath enriched herself are the necessaries of life, and will always have a market while eating is the custom of Europe.

But she has protected us, say some. That she hath engrossed us is true, and defended the continent at our expense as well as her own, is admitted; and she would have defended Turkey from the same motive, *viz.* the sake of trade and dominion.

Alas! we have been long led away by ancient prejudices and made large sacrifices to superstition. We have boasted the protection of Great Britain, without considering, that her motive was *interest* not *attachment*; and that she did not protect us from *our enemies* on *our account,* but from *her enemies* on *her own account,* from those who had no quarrel with us on any *other account,* and who will always be our enemies on the *same account*. Let Britain waive her pretensions to the continent, or the continent throw off the dependance, and we should be at peace with France and Spain, were they at war with Britain. . . .

But Britain is the parent country, say some. Then the more shame upon her conduct. Even brutes do not devour their young, nor savages make war upon their families; wherefore the assertion, if true, turns to her reproach; but it happens not to be true, or only partly so, and the phrase *parent* or *mother country* hath been jesuitically adopted by the king and his parasites, with a low papistical design of gaining an unfair bias on the credulous weakness of our minds. Europe, and not England, is the parent country of America. This new world hath been the asylum for the persecuted lovers of civil and religious liberty from *every part* of Europe. Hither have they fled, not from the tender embraces of the mother, but from the cruelty of the monster; and it is so far true of England, that the same tyranny which drove the first emigrants from home, pursues their

(continued)

descendants still. . . . I challenge the warmest advocate for reconciliation to show a single advantage that this continent can reap by being connected with Great Britain. I repeat the challenge: not a single advantage is derived. Our corn will fetch its price in any market in Europe, and our imported goods must be paid for buy them where we will.

But the injuries and disadvantages which we sustain by that connection, are without number; and our duty to mankind at large, as well as to ourselves, instruct us to renounce the alliance: because, any submission to, or dependance on Great Britain, tends directly to involve this Continent in European wars and quarrels, and sets us at variance with nations who would otherwise seek our friendship, and against whom we have neither anger nor complaint. As Europe is our market for trade, we ought to form no partial connection with any part of it. It is the true interest of America to steer clear of European contentions, which she never can do, while, by her dependance on Britain, she is made the make-weight in the scale of British politics.

Europe is too thickly planted with kingdoms to be long at peace, and whenever a war breaks out between England and any foreign power, the trade of America goes to ruin, *because of her connection with Britain*. The next war may not turn out like the last, and should it not, the advocates for reconciliation now will be wishing for separation then, because neutrality in that case would be a safer convoy than a man of war. Every thing that is right or natural pleads for separation. The blood of the slain, the weeping voice of nature cries, 'TIS TIME TO PART. Even the distance at which the Almighty hath placed England and America is a strong and natural proof that the authority of the one over the other, was never the design of Heaven.

Vocabulary

asserted—stated positively

hath—has

flourished—prospered

fallacious—wrong

thrived—grew well

precedent—an earlier happening that should be a model for later happenings

roundly—in a forceful manner

commerce—trade, business

enriched—made rich

engrossed—occupied

dominion—absolute ownership

motive—something that causes a person to act

pretensions—goals that may not be reached

devour—eat

jesuitically—done in a secret manner

parasites—things dependent on something else for support

papistical—relating to the Catholic Church

bias—prejudice

credulous—ready to believe based on little evidence

asylum—a place of shelter and security

persecuted—bothered by attempts to hurt

civil—relating to citizens

hither—to this place

tyranny—harsh power

emigrants—people who leave a place

advocate—person who argues for something

reconciliation—the act of restoring friendship

fetch—bring

sustain—suffer

renounce—to give up

submission—the condition of giving in to others

variance—state of being in disagreement

contentions—arguments

make-weight—something of little independent value thrown in to fill a gap

pleads—argues

slain—killed

design—plan

Comprehension Questions

1. What argument against independence did Paine consider first? How does he respond to this argument?

2. How does he counter the argument that Britain protected its American colonies?

3. For what, according to Paine, should Britain be ashamed?

4. Who does he say is the parent of America? Why?

5. What does Paine challenge American supporters of the British to do?

6. For what two reasons does Paine think the colonies should separate from Britain?

7. How does Paine think the connection of the American colonies with Britain affects the colonies' relationship with other countries?

8. How does Paine think this connection can affect trade relations?

9. *Note:* As an alternative to questions 1–8, students might list the points made in the discussion in two columns on a sheet of paper entitled "Arguments Against Independence" and "Paine's Response."

Critical Thinking

1. What is the purpose of *Common Sense*?

2. Why do you think Paine chose that title?

3. Paine challenged British loyalists to name one advantage the colonies would have in remaining in the British Empire. Can you think of any?

4. How, according to Paine, would remaining in the British Empire affect the colonies' relations with foreign countries?

5. Paine's language can be very emotional and uses exaggeration. Give some examples of this.

6. Is Paine's style of argument effective? Explain.

Making Connections

1. What other books in history have had a significant effect on public opinion?

2. Paine writes that Europe is more the mother country of the colonies than Britain because Americans have come from many parts of Europe. Do you agree? Why or why not?

3. Paine argues that the colonies would have grown even more economically if it were not for British control. Do you agree? Why or why not?

4. Paine writes that some people argue that Britain has protected its American colonies. To what event is he referring?

5. In another part of *Common Sense,* Paine tells his readers, "A government of our own is our natural right." What other document makes a reference to natural rights?

Relating the Past to Our Lives

1. Have you ever read a book that changed your opinion on something important to you? Explain.

2. Today is it more or less likely for a book to have such an effect on a public issue? Explain.

3. Why does appealing to people's belief in common sense help in a writer's or speaker's argument?

Essay Questions

1. When Paine refers to "our duty to mankind," he seems to suggest that an independent America has a mission in the world. What do you think Paine believes this mission is?

2. Paine argues for no compromise with Britain. Was a compromise possible in 1776? If so, what would it be? If not, why not?

3. How would someone loyal to the British crown respond to *Common Sense*? Were there benefits to remaining a part of the British Empire?

"Remember the Ladies"

Document: Letters between Abigail and John Adams (March–April 1776)

Historical Context

Most women accepted their status in colonial society. This was a system they were born into and they knew no other. But a few women were inspired by the ideas of liberty and equality that men so often spoke about before the Revolution. Abigail Adams was one of these woman. In 1776, Abigail tried to influence her husband, John, about the status of women. She wanted him to consider improving women's position when the time came for a new government to be formed.

A wife's importance before the Revolution was her contribution to her family's well-being. Her domestic work such as spinning and weaving added to household wealth and comfort. Wives often were assistants to their husbands in managing the household. This was especially so when the husband was away. Outside the home, the wife's position, however, was strictly limited. Public participation in politics was off-limits. Educational opportunities were limited as well. Any legal rights a woman had were taken over by her husband upon marriage.

The Revolutionary War seemed to be the right time to advance the cause of women. Arguments for liberty and equality were everywhere. This "contagion of liberty" caused many groups to try to improve their position in society. Women had contributed to and sacrificed for the war. Many served their families and their country by keeping their farms from going broke. Abigail Adams was an excellent example of this. John was away from the family's household in Braintree, Massachusetts, for most of the war.

- He spent most of 1774–1777 in Philadelphia at the First and Second Continental Congresses,

- Through much of 1778–1783, John served overseas as a diplomat in France and Holland.

Abigail kept the farm going despite high taxes and inflated currency. Her letters describe decisions she made under difficult conditions. She saw her oldest son, John Quincy, off to France with his father in February of 1778. She didn't know for months whether they had arrived safely. Through all this, she learned to be a "farmeress" and manage finances.

Importance

Since John and Abigail were often apart, many letters between them exist. Personal letters offer the historian a window into people's lives. Personal letters include issues raised in private that never would be aired in public. Some correspondents lived through compelling historical events while situated well to observe them. These people's letters offer the researcher more than personal details. Such is the case with the Adams's correspondence.

Abigail's March 1776 letter shows an interest in politics. She is anxious to have the Congress declare independence. But the letter also shows dissatisfaction with the position of women. Although others felt this dissatisfaction, few women would express it publicly. Abigail Adams certainly would not. These personal letters also show Abigail and John's relationship. They genuinely enjoy each other.

Note: The language has not been changed. Even though John and Abigail were very smart, their spelling was not good by modern standards. This is because spelling had not really become standardized yet.

Letter from Abigail Adams to John Adams, March 31, 1776

I long to hear that you have declared an independency—and by the way in the new Code of Laws which I suppose it will be necessary for you to make I desire you would Remember the Ladies, and be more generous and favourable to them than your ancestors. Do not put such unlimited power into the hands of the Husbands. Remember all Men would be tyrants if they could. If perticuliar care and attention is not paid to the Laidies we are determined to foment a Rebelion, and will not hold ourselves bound by any Laws in which we have no voice, or Representation.

That your Sex are Naturally Tyrannical is a Truth so thoroughly established as to admit of no dispute, but such of you as wish to be happy willingly give up the harsh title of Master for the more tender and endearing one of Friend. Why then, not put it out of the power of the vicious and the Lawless to use us with cruelty and indignity with impunity. Men of Sense in all Ages abhor those customs which treat us only as the vassals of your Sex. Regard us then as Beings placed by providence under your protection and in immitation of the Supreem Being make use of that power only for our happiness.

[Abigail Adams to John Adams, 31 March–5 April 1776. Adams family papers. Massachusetts Historical Society.]

Letter from John Adams to Abigail Adams, April 14, 1776

As to your extraordinary Code of Laws, I cannot but laugh. We have been told that our Struggle has loosened the bands of Government every where. That Children and Apprentices were disobedient—that schools and Colledges were grown turbulent—that Indians slighted their Guardians and Negroes grew insolent to their Masters.

But your Letter was the first Intimation that another Tribe more numerous and powerfull than all the rest were grown discontented. – This is rather too coarse a Compliment but you are so saucy, I wont blot it out.

Depend upon it, We know better than to repeal our Masculine systems. Altho they are in full Force, you know they are little more than Theory. We dare not exert our Power in its full Latitude. We are obliged to go fair, and softly, and in Practice you know We are the subjects. We have only the Name of Masters, and rather than give up this, which would compleatly subject Us to the Despotism of the Peticoat, I hope General Washington, and all our brave Heroes would fight. I am sure every good Politician would plot, as long as he would against Despotism, Empire, Monarchy, Aristocracy, Oligarchy, or Ochlocracy. – A fine Story indeed. I begin to think the Ministry as deep as they are wicked. After stirring up Tories, Landjobbers, Trimmers, Bigots, Canadians, Indians, Negroes, Hanoverians, Hessians, Russians, Irish Roman Catholicks, Scotch Renegadoes, at last they have stimulated the to demand new Priviledges and threaten to rebell.

[John Adams to Abigail Adams, 14 April 1776. Adams family papers. Masssachusetts Historical Society.]

Vocabulary

tyrants—rulers who use power harshly

foment—to encourage the development of

tyrannical—having the characteristics of a tyrant

dispute—argument

endearing—becoming loved or admired

indignity—an insult; humiliating treatment

impunity—freedom from punishment

abhor—to hate

vassals—servants

providence—God's guidance

apprentices—persons bound to serve others while learning a trade

turbulent—causing unrest or disturbance

insolent—showing boldness and lack of respect

intimation—something made known

saucy—bold or forward

repeal—do away with

latitude—freedom of action or choice

despotism—a system of government in which the ruler has unlimited power

petticoat—woman's skirt; also, women in general

aristocracy—government by a small privileged class

oligarchy—government by a few

ochlocracy—mob rule

landjobbers—dealers in land

trimmers—persons who take the safest political position

Hanoverians—supporters of the British king

Hessians—German soldiers hired by Britain to fight in the colonies

Comprehension Questions

1. What does Abigail want the Continental Congress in Philadelphia to do?

2. When a new government is created, whom does she want to be considered?

3. Who does she fear has "unlimited power"?

4. What does she write may result, if women are ignored?

5. What does she accuse men of "naturally" being?

6. From what kind of men do women need the government's protection?

    7. Does John take his wife's request seriously?

    8. What is his answer to her request?

Critical Thinking

    1. Is Abigail complaining about her relationship with John, or is she speaking for other women? Explain.

    2. What does John mean when he refers to "our Struggle"?

    3. What other groups does he claim have requested more rights due to the Revolution? What do they all have in common?

    4. When John refers to "another tribe," to whom does he refer?

    5. Does John believe men exercise their full power over women?

    6. What does John say is actually the relationship between husband and wife?

Making Connections

    1. How is Abigail's letter influenced by the colonies' relationship with the king?

    2. How typical do you think John's response was for a man at this time?

    3. In what ways did women show their patriotism during the war?

    4. In what ways did women step out of their traditional roles to help the war effort?

Relating the Past to Our Lives

    1. What would Abigail Adams think of women's roles in American society today? Would she approve or not?

    2. Are women treated equally today? Why or why not?

    3. In Abigail Adams's time, men and women had specific areas of life that were considered appropriate for them. For example, men were involved in war and politics. Women dealt with home and children. To what extent have those boundaries been broken today, and to what extent do they still exist?

Essay Questions

    1. Does Abigail want full equality for women? Explain.

    2. What you think about John's attitude? How do you think Abigail felt when reading his response? What do you think Abigail will say in the next letter?

    3. Why is the ability to own property important? What does the right of married women to own property mean for them?

The Declaration of Independence

Document: The Declaration of Independence (1776)

Historical Context

In July 1776, John Adams wrote his wife Abigail, "I am apt to believe that [the day] will be celebrated by succeeding Generations as the great anniversary festival." But Adams was wrong. He meant July 2, when the Second Continental Congress in Philadelphia voted to separate from Great Britain. July 4, our national holiday, celebrates the day the Congress agreed to the Declaration of Independence. This came after two days of debate and language changes. For several years, the colonies had been angry at Great Britain. They were angry about policies that seemed to treat American colonists as less than English citizens. What events caused many to begin to push for the serious step of independence?

- In many ways, the war began in Lexington and Concord on April 19, 1775. Later, on June 17, more blood had been spilled at Bunker Hill.

- In November 1775, the Royalist governor of Virginia promised freedom for all slaves who joined the British cause.

- Thomas Paine's *Common Sense*, calling for independence, was published in January 1776. It caused many members of the public to seriously consider independence.

- Delegates of the middle colonies had been reluctant to support independence. These colonies included Pennsylvania, New York, and New Jersey. King George III refused even to read an offer of compromise called the Olive Branch Petition in 1776. These middle-colony delegates then began to accept separation from Great Britain.

- Independence supporters hoped an official separation from Britain would help the war effort. Generally, diplomatic custom disapproved of one nation's involvement in another's civil war or rebellion. But two separate warring nations could more acceptably get foreign aid. The colonies desperately needed foreign aid. France, an enemy of the British, was one country that might help.

Richard Henry Lee of Virginia proposed an official statement of independence in June 1776. Congress then assigned the job of drafting it to a committee of five. Among its members were Thomas Jefferson, Benjamin Franklin, and John Adams. The committee asked Jefferson to write a first draft. He represented the important state of Virginia. He also had, as Adams said later, a "masterly pen."

The signers were well aware they had just committed treason. Therefore, if the war failed, they had signed their death warrants. Franklin's call for unity said it best: "Gentlemen, we must hang together or surely we will hang separately."

Importance

The Declaration of Independence is one of our nation's two most important founding documents. It is more than just an announcement of our separation from Britain. It states the ideals that the country hopes to live up to even today. It is also a very important statement about our approach to government.

The document begins with a statement of purpose. Then it presents the reason government exists and a government's responsibility to its people. The next part lists examples of why King George III had failed in this responsibility. The final paragraph formally states the colonies' separation from the British Empire.

The Declaration of Independence, 1776

The Unanimous Declaration of the thirteen united States of America

When in the course of human events, it becomes necessary for one people to dissolve the political bands which have connected them with another, and to assume among the powers of the earth, the separate and equal station to which the laws of nature and of nature's God entitle them, a decent respect to the opinions of mankind requires that they should declare the causes which impel them to the separation.

We hold these truths to be self-evident, that all men are created equal, that they are endowed by their Creator with certain unalienable rights, that among these are Life, Liberty and the pursuit of Happiness. —That to secure these rights, governments are instituted among men, deriving their just powers from the consent of the governed. —That whenever any form of government becomes destructive of these ends, it is the right of the people to alter or to abolish it, and to institute new government, laying its foundation on such principles and organizing its powers in such form, as to them shall seem most likely to effect their safety and happiness. . . .

The history of the present King of Great Britain [George III] is a history of repeated injuries and usurpations, all having in direct object the establishment of an absolute Tyranny over these States. To prove this, let Facts be submitted to a candid world. . . .

He has combined with others to subject us to a jurisdiction foreign to our constitution, and unacknowledged by our laws; giving his Assent to their Acts of pretended Legislation:

(continued)

For quartering large bodies of armed troops among us:

For protecting them, by a mock trial, from punishment for any murders which they should commit on the inhabitants of these states:

For cutting off our trade with all parts of the world:

For imposing taxes on us without our consent:

For depriving us in many cases, of the benefits of trial by jury:

For transporting us beyond seas to be tried for pretended offenses:

For abolishing the free system of English laws in a neighboring province, establishing therein an arbitrary government, and enlarging its boundaries so as to render it at once an example and fit instrument for introducing the same absolute rule into these colonies:

For taking away our charters, abolishing our most valuable laws, and altering fundamentally the forms of our governments:

For suspending our own legislatures, and declaring themselves invested with power to legislate for us in all cases whatsoever.

He has abdicated government here, by declaring us out of his protection and waging war against us.

He has plundered our seas, ravaged our coasts, burned our towns, and destroyed the lives of our people.

He is at this time transporting large armies of foreign mercenaries to complete the works of death, desolation and tyranny, already begun with circumstances of cruelty and perfidy scarcely paralleled in the most barbarous ages, and totally unworthy of the head of a civilized nation. . . .

We, therefore, the representatives of the United States of America, in General Congress, assembled, appealing to the Supreme Judge of the world for the rectitude of our intentions, do, in the name, and by the authority of the good people of these colonies, solemnly publish and declare, that these united colonies are, and of right ought to be, free and independent states; that they are absolved from all allegiance to the British Crown, and that all political connection between them and the state of Great Britain, is and ought to be totally dissolved; and that as free and independent states, they have full power to levy war,

(continued)

conclude peace, contract alliances, establish commerce, and to do all other acts and things which independent states may of right do. And for the support of this declaration, with a firm reliance on the protection of Divine Providence, we mutually pledge to each other our lives, our fortunes and our sacred honor.

Vocabulary

political bands—connections with a government

impel—to urge or drive forward

unalienable—not able to be taken away

usurpations—things taken by force

tyranny—oppressive power brought to bear by government

candid—fair

imposing—establishing

abolishing—doing away with

arbitrary—not fixed by law

suspending—stopping temporarily

abdicated—given up power

plundered—taken by force

mercenaries—soldiers hired by a foreign nation

perfidy—a disloyal act

rectitude—the quality of being morally right

absolved—set free from an obligation

allegiance—loyalty

levy—wage, carry on

Comprehension Questions

1. The first sentence can be considered the document's topic sentence.

   • What does this sentence say that the colonies intend to do?

   • What is the document's stated purpose?

2. According to Jefferson, what rights are all people born with? If something is self-evident, does it need to be proven?

3. What can people do, according to the document, if government does not fulfill its responsibilities?

4. In introducing the grievances, Jefferson describes the colonies' experiences with the king. How does he sum up these experiences? What does Jefferson say the king's intention is?

5. The document lists grievances against the king. List three in your own words.

6. In the final statement, the colonies appeal to the "Supreme Judge of the world." To whom are they referring?

7. In your own words, what is the main idea of the first six lines of the Declaration's last paragraph?

8. The last phrase states that "we mutually pledge to each other our lives, our fortunes and our sacred honor." What are the signers saying is at stake?

Critical Thinking

1. The Declaration says that the colonies are dissolving "political bands" with another government. What were the people of the colonies doing when they dissolved "political bands"? Why do the colonies feel they should explain the reasons for this to the world?

2. Why does government exist, according to Jefferson? How do governments acquire their power, according to Jefferson? What does "consent of the governed" mean?

3. Which is most important sentence in the document? Why?

4. Look at the organization of the Declaration of Independence. What component parts make it up? How is it organized like a good essay?

5. To what extent would you call the signers of the Declaration of Independence courageous? Why?

Making Connections

1. Why was it necessary to make a formal declaration in this case? Can you think of other occasions in which a formal declaration is necessary?

2. Find the grievances mentioned in the Declaration that match the following events:

The Coercive (or Intolerable) Acts

The Quartering Acts

The Admiralty Courts for smuggling

The Quebec Act

No taxation without representation

The hiring of Hessians to fight in the war

3. Lines 9 through 11 of the Declaration's last paragraph list some rights of independent countries. What other rights do sovereign nations have?

Relating the Past to Our Lives

1. Independence can be both exciting and frightening. Why? Can you think of an instance when you began something on your own for the first time? Describe your emotions at the outset of the activity.

2. Jefferson identified three natural rights in the Declaration: "Life, Liberty and the pursuit of Happiness." What do these specifically refer to in people's lives today? List them.

3. What does the Fourth of July mean to you?

Essay Questions

1. In what ways was the "all men are created equal" phrase more of an ideal than a reality in 1776? What basic inequalities existed among races and genders then? To what extent have we lived up to those ideals today? In what ways have we fallen short?

2. The Declaration states that a government's powers come from the "consent of the governed." What responsibilities does that place on the people? In your opinion, how are the American people living up to those responsibilities today?

3. The document begins, "The Unanimous Declaration of the thirteen united States of America." What was the Congress's intention in using this subtitle? Would it have been possible to declare independence without unanimous consent of all the colonies? If so, what problem(s) might that present?

4. The Declaration of Independence has been called a timeless document. This means it is relevant beyond its time period. It has also been a model for other nations. What makes it timeless and applicable to other nations? What makes the Declaration a radical statement?

Slave Journey

Document: Olaudah Equiano, *The Interesting Narrative of the Life of Olaudah Equiano, or Gustavus Vasa, The African, Written by Himself* (1789)

Historical Context

Nightmarish is a word that should be used to describe the Middle Passage from an African's point of view. This voyage was the second part of a system of triangular trade. One example of this three-way trade would be as follows:

- A ship carrying British cloth, firearms, and American rum would sail from the colonies to Africa. This cargo was traded for African slaves.

- Packed with slaves, the ship then sailed to the West Indies sugar islands. There, the ship exchanged its cargo for sugar and molasses. Many slaves would be "seasoned" in the West Indies to prepare them for the American colonies.

- The sugar and molasses were shipped to the New England colonies to be converted into rum.

For the slaves the 3,700-mile journey from Africa's West Coast must have been frightening and hellish. Partly, the fear came from the unknown. The captives were usually kidnapped by another African ethnic group. They traveled from the interior to holding cells in large forts built along the coast. There, they waited for the arrival of slave ships. Once aboard, the Africans could not imagine what lay ahead. Some thought they would be killed. Others thought, as Equiano Olaudah did, that the whites planned to eat them. No Africans ever returned to explain. From 1700 to 1810, ships carried seven million slaves to North and South America. Of those, about 500,000 ended up in North America.

Once aboard, the slaves lived under horrible conditions. The ship captain crammed three to four hundred passengers below deck linked by chains. Health conditions were terrible. The tight living conditions combined with sweltering temperatures lead to the rapid spread of infectious diseases. Because the slaves were chained together while kept below, buckets were used for human waste. The stench from these buckets could be sickening. The Africans on board usually came from a variety of ethnic groups in Africa and could not converse in the same language. Many Africans became depressed and refused to eat. But they were forced to eat against their will, because they were now worth money. On average, about 10 to 15 percent of slave ship captives died during the voyage to the Americas.

Importance

Olaudah Equiano's was the first-ever autobiography of a freed slave. That it describes aspects of slave life not included in later slave narratives makes the book even more rare.

Ex-slaves, such as Frederick Douglass, wrote narratives in the nineteenth century. But these authors were born in the United States. Equiano's descriptions of his capture in Africa and the Middle Passage are unique. At eleven years old in 1745, Equiano was taken from his Igbo village in what is northeast Nigeria today. After he landed in the West Indies, he was sold to a Virginia planter. A British captain later purchased him. Eventually Equiano purchased his freedom and lived in England. There, he became an important figure in the British abolitionist movement. His book was published in 1789.

Olaudah Equiano, *The Interesting Narrative of the Life of Olaudah Equiano, or Gustavus Vasa, the African, Written by Himself,* 1789

The first object which saluted my eyes when I arrived on the coast was the sea, and a slave ship, which was then riding at anchor, and waiting for its cargo. These filled me with astonishment, which was soon converted into terror, when I was carried on board. . . .

At last, when the ship we were in had got in all her cargo, they made ready with many fearful noises, and we were all put under deck, so that we could not see how they managed the vessel. But this disappointment was the least of my sorrow. The stench of the hold while we were on the coast was so intolerably loathsome, that it was dangerous to remain there for any time, and some of us had been permitted to stay on the deck for the fresh air; but now that the whole ship's cargo were confined together, it became absolutely pestilential. The closeness of the place, and the heat of the climate, added to the number in the ship, which was so crowded that each had scarcely room to turn himself, almost suffocated us. This produced copious perspirations, so that the air soon became unfit for respiration, from a variety of loathsome smells, and brought on a sickness among the slaves, of which many died, thus falling victims to the improvident avarice, as I may call it, of their purchasers. This wretched situation was again aggravated by the galling of the chains, now become insupportable; and the filth of the necessary tubs, into which the children often fell, and were almost suffocated. The shrieks of the women, and the groans of the dying, rendered the whole a scene of horror almost inconceivable. Happily perhaps for myself I was soon reduced so low here that it was thought necessary to keep me almost always on deck; and from my extreme youth I was not put in fetters. . . .

(continued)

One day, when we had a smooth sea and moderate wind, two of my wearied countrymen who were chained together (I was near them at the time), preferring death to such a life of misery, somehow made through the nettings and jumped into the sea: immediately another quite dejected fellow, who, on account of his illness, was suffered to be out of irons, also followed their example; and I believe many more would very soon have done the same if they had not been prevented by the ship's crew, who were instantly alarmed. Those of us that were the most active were in a moment put down under the deck, and there was such a noise and confusion amongst the people of the ship as I never heard before, to stop her, and get the boat out to go after the slaves. However two of the wretches were drowned, but they got the other, and afterwards flogged him unmercifully for thus attempting to prefer death to slavery. In this manner we continued to undergo more hardships than I can now relate, hardships which are inseparable from this accursed trade. . . .

At last we came in sight of the island of Barbadoes, at which the whites on board gave a great shout, and made many signs of joy to us; but as the vessel drew nearer, we plainly saw the harbour, and other ships of different kinds and sizes; and we soon anchored amongst them, off Bridge Town. Many merchants and planters now came on board, though it was in the evening. They put us in separate parcels, and examined us attentively. They also made us jump, and pointed to the land, signifying we were to go there.

Vocabulary

saluted—became apparent to

converted—turned

stench—stink

hold—inside the ship belowdecks

loathsome—disgusting

confined—held within a location

pestilential—causing infectious disease

closeness—condition of having no openings

copious perspirations—large quantities of sweat

respiration—breathing

improvident avarice—thoughtless, uneconomic greed

aggravated—made worse

galling—making sore by rubbing

inconceivable—unbelievable

reduced so low—depressed

fetters—chains

moderate—average

dejected—sad

suffered—allowed

wretches—miserable people

flogged—whipped

accursed—very bad

vessel—ship

parcels—groups

attentively—carefully

signifying—showing

Comprehension Questions

1. What did Equiano see when he was brought to the coast?

2. Where in the ship were the slaves housed?

3. What did Equiano first notice when he went down to the hold?

4. What conditions caused the Africans to sweat?

5. What conditions led to slaves' deaths?

6. Why was Equiano mostly not in chains?

7. Why did some of the Africans try to kill themselves by jumping overboard?

8. What happened to the slaves who jumped?

9. Where did the ship land?

10. Once the ship arrived, who boarded it to inspect the Africans?

Critical Thinking

1. Why was Equiano astonished by the sight of the ship?

2. Equiano earlier wrote that he really believed that he was going to be eaten at the end of the voyage. Why would he think this?

3. What were the "necessary tubs"?

4. Why was the man who jumped into the water to commit suicide flogged when he was rescued?

5. Why did the merchants and planters examine the Africans and make them jump?

Making Connections

1. The West Indies sugar islands had the highest slave death rate. Why do you think that was?

2. When slaves on the voyage refused food, they were forced to eat. Why would the slave ship's crew force its captives to eat?

3. Get a world map. Find Nigeria in Africa. Trace Equiano's route from his home village to the coast of Africa to Barbados to Virginia.

Relating the Past to Our Lives

1. Imagine yourself in Equiano's position upon boarding the slave ship. Remember, he was eleven years old. How would you have felt? What would you have done?

2. Slavery itself ended in Great Britain's colonies in 1834 and in the United States in 1865. Do other similar evils exist today that people are trying to eliminate?

3. To survive his ordeal and eventually purchase his freedom, what qualities must Equiano have possessed?

Essay Questions

1. Equiano wrote of these experiences about thirty years after they happened. How might that have affected his story?

2. The autobiography was very popular when it first came out in 1789. Why do you think it was so popular?

3. Seven million or more of Africa's inhabitants were taken away over a hundred-year span. What kind of effect do you think this had on the people left behind in Africa?

Document: J. Hector St. John de Crèvecoeur, "What Is an American?" (1782)

Historical Context

What is an American? This would be an interesting question to consider today. It was even more interesting 250 years ago. The United States had recently won the world's first colonial war for independence and promised to create a society different from any other. J. Hector St. John de Crèvecoeur was the first writer to try publicly to describe this new nationality, an American. His description was included in his book *Letters from an American Farmer*. It was published in 1782, the year before the Revolutionary War ended.

Crèvecoeur was born in France. He came to the American colonies in 1754 at the age of nineteen. He first worked as a land surveyor and peddler, a sort of traveling salesman. These jobs required that he travel within the interior of the colonies. He believed his time spent in the wilderness helped him learn a great deal about the American colonies and people. As a foreigner, he was perhaps well suited to compare what he saw with European society. In 1765, Crèvecoeur settled in New York, where he became a citizen and farmer. He married an American woman, the daughter of a merchant.

Importance

This early statement focuses on what made America unique. Crèvecoeur began writing the book when he settled in New York in 1765. So his observations are of colonial American society. He notes the colonies' ethnic diversity, their lack of social class divisions, and the opportunity the colonies present for poor immigrants. Many readers at the time believed he was overly positive in his description. They thought he exaggerated the good parts of American culture, presenting it as a utopia. Today we might view him as an early promoter of what became known as the "American Dream." Crèvecoeur did not consider the lives of slaves or the fate of the Indians, however. Most people at the time shared this lack of concern. *Letters from an American Farmer* sold well all over Europe. For many, it was the only impression they had of this new nation. For us today, it is a great opportunity to see how well our present society has lived up to the ideals of Crèvecoeur's American Dream.

J. Hector St. John de Crèvecoeur, *Letters from an American Farmer*, 1782
"Letter III—What Is an American?"

He is arrived on a new continent; a modern society offers itself to his contemplation, different from what he had hitherto seen. It is not composed, as in Europe, of great lords who possess every thing, and of a herd of people who have nothing. Here are no aristocratical families, no courts, no kings, no bishops, no ecclesiastical dominion, no invisible power giving to a few a very visible one; no great manufacturers employing thousands, no great refinements of luxury. The rich and the poor are not so far removed from each other as they are in Europe. . . .

What then is the American, this new man? He is either an European, or the descendant of an European, hence that strange mixture of blood, which you will find in no other country. I could point out to you a family whose grandfather was an Englishman, whose wife was Dutch, whose son married a French woman, and whose present four sons have now four wives of different nations. He is an American, who, leaving behind him all his ancient prejudices and manners, receives new ones from the new mode of life he has embraced, the new government he obeys, and the new rank he holds. He becomes an American by being received in the broad lap of our great Alma Mater.

Here individuals of all nations are melted into a new race of men, whose labours and posterity will one day cause great changes in the world. . . . The Americans were once scattered all over Europe; here they are incorporated into one of the finest systems of population which has ever appeared, and which will hereafter become distinct by the power of the different climates they inhabit. The American ought therefore to love this country much better than that wherein either he or his forefathers were born. Here the rewards of his industry follow with equal steps the progress of his labour; . . . Wives and children, who before in vain demanded of him a morsel of bread, now, fat and frolicsome, gladly help their father to clear those fields whence exuberant crops are to arise to feed and to clothe them all; without any part being claimed, either by a despotic prince, a rich abbot, or a mighty lord. . . . The American is a new man, who acts upon new principles; he must therefore entertain new ideas, and form new opinions. From involuntary idleness, servile dependence, penury, and useless labour, he has passed to toils of a very different nature, rewarded by ample subsistence. — This is an American.

 www.socialstudies.com/walch

Vocabulary

contemplation—consideration

hitherto—up to this time

aristocratical—upper-class

ecclesiastical—relating to a church

refinements—elegance

descendant—offspring

Alma Mater—Latin for "caring mother"

posterity—future generations

incorporated—united

hereafter—in the future

distinct—different

wherein—where

industry—hard work

in vain—without success

frolicsome—playful

whence—from a source

exuberant—plentiful

despotic—exercising absolute power

abbot—the head of a monastery of monks

involuntary—without choice

idleness—inactivity

servile—extremely obedient

penury—severe poverty

ample—plentiful

subsistence—what is needed to support life, such as food and shelter

Comprehension Questions

1. What does Crèvecoeur find missing from American society that is present in European societies?

2. The people of the American colonies came from mainly what continent?

3. What example does Crèvecoeur give to show the variety of nations from which the American population began?

4. What causes these former Europeans to change after arriving here?

5. Once here, what do all of these different nationalities melt together to become?

6. In America, what results from hard work, according to Crèvecoeur?

7. In Europe, what could happen to the crops a farmer grew?

8. According to Crèvecoeur, American life leads to what changes in this new man's thinking?

Critical Thinking

1. What does Crèvecoeur mean when he writes "the rich and the poor are not so far removed from each other"?

2. According to Crèvecoeur, why is America the land of opportunity?

3. Crèvecoeur compares life in America with life in Europe. What problems does Crèvecoeur describe in European society?

4. Crèvecoeur implies that once here an immigrant leaves behind, perhaps not immediately, those "ancient prejudices and manners." Do you think that will happen? Why or why not?

5. What overall point do you think Crèvecoeur is trying to make in this excerpt?

6. Does he give too optimistic an impression? Explain.

Making Connections

1. Crèvecoeur describes his ideas about the mixture of national groups in America. How are those ideas different from or similar to the later "melting pot" theory of this mixing?

2. Why do you think Crèvecoeur ignores African Americans and Native Americans in his description of an American?

3. Crèvecoeur writes that among American people there were not great differences in wealth. Why do you think that was?

Relating the Past to Our Lives

1. Crèvecoeur believes that starting over in a new place can change people. Do you think that is true? Explain.

2. In your experience, does hard work always pay off?

3. What immigrant groups make up your ancestry? Do you consider yourself a full-fledged American?

4. Today, future American citizens still arrive from different parts of the world. Europe is still represented. From what other continents and countries do immigrants come?

5. Do you think today's immigrants melt together into Americans? Explain.

Essay Questions

1. Crèvecoeur sees Americans becoming "distinct by the power of the different climates they inhabit"? Do you believe that geographical region has a large influence on differences among people in the United States? Explain.

2. Crèvecoeur's omission of certain groups, such as slaves and Native Americans, shows a lot about colonial society. In what ways has American society improved since then? In what ways does it need to improve further?

3. What is the difference between the immigrant experience now and in Crèvecoeur's time? What is similar?

George Washington's Farewell Address

Document: George Washington, Farewell Address (1796)

Historical Context

The Twenty-second Amendment to the U.S. Constitution became law in 1951. It limits a U.S. president to two terms. Until Franklin Roosevelt in 1940, no president had won a third term. Only a few tried. President George Washington began the two-term tradition. Almost all later presidents held to this tradition.

Washington's departure from office was also important for his final speech, or address, to the American people. By the end of his second term in 1796, Washington had had enough of politics. Sixty-four was a reasonable age to retire from public life. He had accepted his second term with reluctance. His health had been declining. He had been away from Mount Vernon, his Virginia plantation, for the better part of eight years. Before that, he had served as the commanding general of the Continental Army from 1775 to 1783.

In addition, Washington had begun to find the presidency less appealing. He had watched political parties develop during his second term. His secretary of the treasury, Alexander Hamilton, led the Federalists. His former secretary of state, Thomas Jefferson, became the Republican leader. Strong competition existed between these two men. Each believed that the other's ideas would harm the country's future. President Washington tried to stay out of the conflict. But he had become identified with the Federalists by the end of his second term.

The Republicans began criticizing Washington. The most important was over Jay's Treaty with England. The Federalists supported this treaty. The pro-French Republicans opposed it. The experience left Washington, a man quite sensitive to criticism, wishing for retirement at Mount Vernon.

These political problems led President Washington to worry about the nation's future. Before leaving office he gave some advice to his country. He called this advice the "warning of a parting friend." Alexander Hamilton wrote a draft of the Farewell Address, and Washington revised it. The address especially concerned two issues that had created conflict during his administrations and threatened future ones. These issues were:

- The quarrels advanced by political parties. At the time, people like Washington believed that political parties were harmful to a nation. They saw political parties as acting for their own self-interest rather than for the well-being of the whole nation.

- Interference by other nations with the affairs of the United States. Washington had his experience with France in mind. It had meddled in American internal politics to get support for its conflict with England.

Importance

This is one of two famous farewell addresses by American presidents. Both included warnings. The other, by Dwight Eisenhower, warned about the growing military-industrial complex. Washington's warnings are interesting today because we have not followed his advice. Some believe these problems cause trouble today. The address is also an interesting look at American thinking at the time, when anything seemed possible. The address has been read in the U.S. Senate on Washington's birthday since 1893.

George Washington, Farewell Address, 1796

Friends and Fellow Citizens:

The period for a new election of a citizen to administer the executive government of the United States being not far distant, and the time actually arrived when your thoughts must be employed in designating the person who is to be clothed with that important trust, it appears to me proper, especially as it may conduce to a more distinct expression of the public voice, that I should now apprise you of the resolution I have formed, to decline being considered among the number of those out of whom a choice is to be made. . . .

I have already intimated to you the danger of parties in the State, with particular reference to the founding of them on geographical discriminations. Let me now take a more comprehensive view, and warn you in the most solemn manner against the baneful effects of the spirit of party generally. . . .

It serves always to distract the public councils and enfeeble the public administration. It agitates the community with ill-founded jealousies and false alarms, kindles the animosity of one part against another, foments occasionally riot and insurrection. It opens the door to foreign influence and corruption . . .

The great rule of conduct for us in regard to foreign nations is in extending our commercial relations, to have with them as little political connection as possible. So far as we have already formed engagements, let them be fulfilled with perfect good faith. Here let us stop. . . .

It is our true policy to steer clear of permanent alliances with any portion of the foreign world; so far, I mean, as we are now at liberty to do it; for let me not be understood as capable of patronizing infidelity to

(continued)

existing engagements. I hold the maxim no less applicable to public than to private affairs, that honesty is always the best policy. I repeat, therefore, let those engagements be observed in their genuine sense. But, in my opinion, it is unnecessary and would be unwise to extend them. . . .

Taking care always to keep ourselves by suitable establishments on a respectable defensive posture, we may safely trust to temporary alliances for extraordinary emergencies. . . .

United States
19th September, 1796
Geo. Washington

Vocabulary

administer—to supervise

executive—the branch of government responsible for carrying out laws; the U.S. president

designating—selecting

trust—responsibility

conduce—lead

distinct—separate

apprise—inform

resolution—firm decision

intimated—made known

discriminations—differences

comprehensive—complete

solemn—serious

baneful—seriously harmful

councils—elected bodies

enfeeble—weaken

agitates—excites

ill-founded—without a sound basis

kindles—stirs up

animosity—hatred

foments—incites, stirs up

insurrection—rebellion against government

corruption—dishonesty

conduct—behavior

commercial—having to do with business

good faith—honesty

alliances—associations between nations

portion—part

patronizing—supporting

infidelity—unfaithfulness

engagements—agreements

maxim—a basic principle

genuine—real

suitable establishments—proper military organizations

Comprehension Questions

1. Who is the intended audience for Washington's address?

2. An election will be held soon. What office will people be voting for?

3. What does Washington say his role will be in that election?

4. What negative effects of political parties does Washington list?

5. Under what circumstances does Washington believe the United States should have relations with foreign nations?

6. What type of relations should the United States avoid?

7. Washington warns against permanent alliances with foreign nations. What exception does he make?

Critical Thinking

1. What do political parties and involvement with foreign nations have in common, according to Washington?

2. Is Washington against relations with foreign countries? Explain.

3. Do you think it was important for Washington to make this address? Explain.

4. Do you think the public, when reading this address, felt more anxious or more comfortable about the future?

Making Connections

1. What is Washington referring to when he writes about parties based on "geographical discriminations"?

2. What would Washington think of NATO? What would he think of the permanent establishment of the political parties?

3. Why is Washington's decision not to run for a third term important?

4. What events during Washington's administrations may have caused him to give the advice he gave?

Relating the Past to Our Lives

1. George Washington was the closest the new nation had to a father. Do you listen to advice from either of your parents? Explain.

2. Washington did not have an outlet for this address when he wrote it. He eventually asked a Philadelphia newspaper to print it. How would he make it public today?

3. Write a farewell address for the current U.S. president, issuing warnings about problems you see that threaten the nation's future in the twenty-first century.

Essay Questions

1. How well are we following Washington's advice? Explain.

2. If we followed Washington's advice today, would the United States be better off or weaker? Explain.

3. Do political parties serve a purpose or simply create more problems? Explain.

The Louisiana Purchase

Document: Letter from Thomas Jefferson to Robert Livingston (1802)

Historical Context

The United States purchased the Louisiana Territory from France in 1803. This purchase doubled the nation's size for $15 million, or four cents an acre. With inflation, the price today would be $190 million. That's still quite a bargain, considering that the land makes up one fourth of the United States today. How did the largest land deal in history happen?

U.S. policy makers had always worried about foreign control of the Mississippi River and the city at its mouth, New Orleans. Farmers west of the Appalachian Mountains relied on the Mississippi to transport their goods to eastern markets. They floated produce on flatboats along rivers that emptied into the Mississippi. The boats then continued down the great river to New Orleans. There the goods were stored to await loading onto an ocean-going ship. This vessel would carry the goods into the Gulf of Mexico. The ship would then sail north along the Atlantic coast to the eastern states. Overland travel was too difficult and costly. There were no easily passable roads through the Appalachian Mountains to get to the East. So access to New Orleans was crucial.

In 1795, the United States had negotiated a treaty with Spain, which then owned the Louisiana Territory. This treaty allowed American farmers to use New Orleans for shipping. Before the treaty, western farmers had threatened to break away from the United States to join Spanish territory if they were kept out of New Orleans. In 1800, that fear arose again. Americans learned that Spain had secretly transferred the Louisiana Territory to France. The 1795 treaty did not apply to France. Also, France under Napoleon Bonaparte was much more powerful and aggressive than Spain was.

Robert R. Livingston was the U.S. minister in France at this time. In 1802, President Thomas Jefferson told Livingston to try to buy New Orleans and some land around it from France for as much as $10 million. In April 1803, Napoleon offered a better deal—all of the Louisiana Territory for $15 million. Why did he do this?

- Napoleon had earlier desired an empire in North America. The disastrous failure of his army to put down a revolt of slaves and free blacks on Haiti led him to reconsider.

- A war between Great Britain and France now seemed unavoidable. Napoleon would need more funds to wage that war.

Livingston and James Monroe, who had joined him in France, did not know what to do. They were not authorized to make the larger purchase. But to get permission from Jefferson would take months. Therefore, they took a chance and accepted the offer. Jefferson was pleased. Not only did the deal give the United States New Orleans, but it also provided the country with room to grow. Acres of new land to the west fit Jefferson's vision of a nation of farmers.

One problem presented itself. Jefferson had previously argued for limited presidential powers. Nothing in the Constitution stated that the president could purchase land. Jefferson stretched his power by buying land. He simply called the deal a treaty, since the Constitution did allow the president to make treaties. Treaties have to be approved by the Senate, which did so on October 20, 1803.

In 1803, Jefferson named Meriwether Lewis and William Clark to head an expedition. Their task was to explore the newly acquired territory. The members of the expedition recorded information on plants and animals. They also informed the Indians in the area that they lived now under an American flag.

Importance

Jefferson wrote the following letter before Napoleon's offer of the entire territory. Since the letter was addressed to Livingston, you would think he was the intended audience. But historians note that the letter was given for delivery, unsealed, to a friend of Jefferson's. Perhaps Jefferson hoped Napoleon would read it, since it included some threats that might help in negotiating a purchase. Regardless, the letter presents a clear statement of U.S. interests concerning the Mississippi River and New Orleans.

Letter from Thomas Jefferson to Robert Livingston, April 18, 1802

Washington, Apr. 18, 1802.

The cession of Louisiana and the Floridas by Spain to France works most sorely on the U. S. . . . It compleatly reverses all the political relations of the U. S. and will form a new epoch in our political course. Of all nations of any consideration France is the one which hitherto has offered the fewest points on which we could have any conflict of right, and the most points of a communion of interests. From these causes we have ever looked to her as our *natural friend,* as one with which we never could have an occasion of difference. Her growth therefore we viewed as our own, her misfortunes ours. There is on the globe one single spot, possessor of which is our natural and habitual enemy. It is New Orleans, through which the produce of three-eighths of our territory must pass to market, and from its fertility it will ere long yield more than half of our whole produce and contain more than half our inhabitants. France

(continued)

placing herself in that door assumes to us the attitude of defiance. Spain might have retained it quietly for years. Her pacific dispositions, her feeble state, would induce her to increase our facilities there, so that her possession of the place would be hardly felt by us, and it would not perhaps be very long before some circumstance might arise which might make the cession of it to us the price of something of more worth to her. Not so can it ever be in the hands of France. The impetuosity of her temper, the energy and restlessness of her character, placed in a point of eternal friction with us, and our character, which though quiet, and loving peace and the pursuit of wealth, is high-minded, despising wealth in competition with insult or injury, enterprising and energetic as any nation on earth, these circumstances render it impossible that France and the U. S. can continue long friends when they meet in so irritable a position. They as well as we must be blind if they do not see this; and we must be very improvident if we do not begin to make arrangements on that hypothesis. The day that France takes possession of N. Orleans fixes the sentence which is to restrain her forever within her low water mark. It seals the union of two nations who in conjunction can maintain exclusive possession of the ocean. From that moment we must marry ourselves to the British fleet and nation. We must turn all our attentions to a maritime force, for which our resources place us on very high grounds: . . . This is not a state of things we seek or desire. It is one which this measure, if adopted by France, forces on us, as necessarily as any other cause, by the laws of nature, brings on its necessary effect.

If France considers Louisiana however as indispensable for her views she might perhaps be willing to look about for arrangements which might reconcile it to our interests. If anything could do this it would be the ceding to us the island of New Orleans and the Floridas. This would certainly in a great degree remove the causes of jarring and irritation between us, and perhaps for such a length of time as might produce other means of making the measure permanently conciliatory to our interests and friendships.

Vocabulary

cession—giving

sorely—painfully

epoch—a time marked by an event beginning a new period

hitherto—up to this time

communion—sharing

misfortunes—bad luck

possessor—owner

habitual—regular

fertility—capability for producing crops

ere—before

defiance—challenge

pacific disposition—peaceful tendencies

feeble—weak

induce—to persuade

facilities—warehouses (in this case)

impetuosity—the quality of reacting without thinking

eternal friction—endless problems

enterprising—ready to experiment

render—to make

improvident—not providing for the future

hypothesis—something accepted for the sake of argument

in conjunction—together

indispensable—absolutely necessary

reconcile—to cause to accept

ceding—giving (but not for free in this case)

jarring—affecting in a negative way

conciliatory—capable of existing in harmony

Comprehension Questions

1. What kind of document is this? To whom is it written?

2. What recent event mentioned in the letter is bad for the United States?

3. What had been the previous relationship of the United States with France, according to Jefferson?

4. What makes France now a natural enemy?

5. Why had the previous Spanish control of New Orleans not been a problem?

6. How is France different from Spain?

7. According to Jefferson, when France takes over New Orleans, what must the United States do?

8. What does Jefferson hope France is willing to do, even if it keeps the Louisiana Territory?

Critical Thinking

1. What is the letter's main idea?

2. List one piece of evidence that indicates how serious a problem Jefferson thinks France's possession of New Orleans is.

3. What do you think of Jefferson's comparison between Spain and France? Is it fair?

4. Because the letter was unsealed, some historians believe that Jefferson hoped that Napoleon would read it. What parts of the letter could indicate that Jefferson might expect an audience broader than Livingston?

Making Connections

1. Why would Jefferson consider France a "natural friend"?

2. How might American history be different if France had sold New Orleans, allowed American farmers to use the Mississippi River, but kept the rest of the Louisiana Territory?

3. For the many Indian tribes that occupied the Louisiana Territory, what did the U.S. purchase mean?

4. Why was it important for Americans to have available land in the West?

Relating the Past to Our Lives

1. Find a map of the Louisiana Territory and a map of the United States today. How many states today came from land included in the Territory? Name them.

2. How is diplomacy between nations today different from that of Jefferson's time?

3. Have you ever had to make an important decision with long-term consequences without much guidance? What factors became part of your decision-making process?

Essay Questions

1. In what ways did the Louisiana Territory benefit the United States? In what ways did it cause problems?

2. With the Louisiana Purchase, Jefferson seemed to act against his belief in limited presidential powers. Why do you think he did this?

3. Do you think Jefferson was bluffing about an alliance with the British against the French? Explain.

The Monroe Doctrine

Document: James Monroe, seventh annual message to Congress (1823)

Historical Context

Given the world status of the United States in 1823, the Monroe Doctrine was a bold statement. The nation was not a great power. It had no standing army and little industry. Nevertheless, President James Monroe's annual message to Congress contained clear warnings to powerful European nations about interference with affairs in the Americas.

Secretary of State John Quincy Adams played a leading part in this policy's development. Adams had made a case for it earlier. He helped with its wording. The doctrine made clear the U.S. policy about Europe's relationship with the Western Hemisphere.

• Europe should no longer consider the Western Hemisphere—North and South America—open for future colonization. The United States will accept already established European colonies in the Americas.

• Europe should also stay out of the political affairs of independent nations within the hemisphere.

• The United States will not involve itself in the political affairs of Europe.

Two issues prompted this statement at the time.

• In 1821, the Russian czar had claimed land south to the fifty-first parallel (now British Columbia). Secretary of State Adams refused to recognize this claim. In his refusal, he made a statement similar to the Monroe Doctrine about the Russian colonization.

• More important, several Central and South American countries had recently won their independence from Spain. They were able to do this while Spain was fighting the Napoleonic Wars in Europe. These new nations had set up republican governments. Adams and Monroe feared that Spain and France might try to recolonize them.

England was a key supporter of the Monroe Doctrine. Once they were no longer colonies, the newly independent Central and South American countries could trade with England. The British, therefore, had an economic interest in keeping its trading partners. In fact, England wanted to issue the doctrine jointly with the United States. But Adams convinced President Monroe that the United States should state the policy alone. He knew that England would still support the policy statement because of its trade interests.

In the decades that followed, Europe ignored the Monroe Doctrine. From time to time, it involved itself in the politics of Latin American countries in minor ways. When that happened, the United States did not mention the Monroe Doctrine. The United States did not use the doctrine until 1890. Then, it became a key part of U.S. foreign policy.

Importance

The Monroe Doctrine is one of two important U.S. foreign policy statements before the Civil War. The other, Washington's Farewell Address, had a similar message—keep Europe out of American affairs. Both policies reflect a U.S. fear at the time—that the "Old World" with its monarchies would corrupt the republican "New World." Europe did not threaten the United States itself. Yet the United States viewed the presence of Old World ideas in the hemisphere as a threat. President Theodore Roosevelt added his famous corollary to the Monroe Doctrine in 1904. It stated that the United States would ensure the stability of Latin American nations. This extended policy led to repeated U.S. intervention in Latin America.

James Monroe, Seventh Annual Message to Congress, December 2, 1823

. . . [T]he American continents, by the free and independent condition which they have assumed and maintain, are henceforth not to be considered as subjects for future colonization by any European powers. . . .

In the wars of the European powers in matters relating to themselves we have never taken any part, nor does it comport with our policy to do so. It is only when our rights are invaded or seriously menaced that we resent injuries or make preparation for our defense. With the movements in this hemisphere we are of necessity more immediately connected, and by causes which must be obvious to all enlightened and impartial observers. The political system of the allied powers is essentially different in this respect from that of America. . . . We owe it, therefore, to candor and to the amicable relations existing between the United States and those powers to declare that we should consider any attempt on their part to extend their system to any portion of this hemisphere as dangerous to our peace and safety. With the existing colonies or dependencies of any European power we have not interfered and shall not interfere. But with the Governments who have declared their independence and maintain it, and whose independence we have, on great consideration and on just principles, acknowledged, we could not view any interposition for the purpose of oppressing them, or controlling in any other manner their destiny, by any European power in any other light than as the manifestation of an unfriendly disposition toward the United States. . . .

(continued)

Our policy in regard to Europe, which was adopted at an early stage of the wars which have so long agitated that quarter of the globe, nevertheless remains the same, which is, not to interfere in the internal concerns of any of its powers; to consider the government de facto as the legitimate government for us; . . .

It is impossible that the allied powers should extend their political system to any portion of either continent without endangering our peace and happiness; . . . It is still the true policy of the United States to leave the parties to themselves, in hope that other powers will pursue the same course.

Vocabulary

henceforth—from now on

comport—fit

menaced—endangered

resent—feel annoyance at

hemisphere—half of the earth; in this case the Western Hemisphere, which includes North and South America

impartial—fair; not biased

allied powers—countries linked by an agreement for a purpose

candor—honesty

amicable—friendly

portion—part

dependencies—countries under the control of, but not part of, other countries

principles—rules or codes of conduct

acknowledged—recognized as true

interposition—the act of getting in the way of

oppressing—crushing with power of authority

manifestation—an act of making apparent

disposition—attitude toward

de facto—in reality

legitimate—lawful

parties—groups taking part in an action or affair

Comprehension Questions

1. What does Monroe warn European countries against doing?

2. In what way has the United States remained out of European affairs up until this time?

3. Under what conditions would the United States prepare to defend itself?

4. To what part of the world is the United States most connected?

5. How are the "allied powers" (European nations) different from the United States?

6. What actions on Europe's part would the United States consider dangerous to it?

7. What will be Monroe's policy regarding already existing European colonies in the Western Hemisphere?

8. Monroe warns European powers against doing what with new independent countries in the Western Hemisphere?

9. What will U.S. policy be toward Europe?

Critical Thinking

1. Why do you think the United States left already existing colonies in the Americas out of its warning to European countries?

2. When Monroe says that our political system is different from that of European countries, what does he mean?

3. Why was it important for Monroe to emphasize that the United States never interfered with the affairs of European countries?

4. How do you think the United States intended to enforce the Monroe Doctrine—or did it?

5. How was the doctrine phrased in ways to be firm but not offensive?

Making Connections

1. How do you think Latin American countries felt about the Monroe Doctrine?

2. Why does the United States fear European involvement in Central and South America?

3. Is the United States declaring its isolation from Europe? If not, how would you describe the policy?

4. Monroe's doctrine was written as part of his annual message to Congress, today's State of the Union Address. Is that a good time to make such a statement? Why or why not?

Relating the Past to Our Lives

1. Do you think it is important for people to make themselves clear about what is acceptable and what is off limits? When have you done that?

2. Many people who know about the Monroe Doctrine do not realize the role John Quincy Adams played in its development. Have you ever been part of a project and not gotten credit? Did it matter to you?

3. Has the current U.S. president made a foreign policy statement of significance perhaps to later generations? If so, what was it?

Essay Questions

1. Compare Washington's warning against forming permanent alliances with the Monroe Doctrine. How are they similar? How are they the different?

2. The Monroe Doctrine is still believed to be in effect. Should it be? Explain.

3. How have advances in transportation, communication, and weapons made foreign policy different from foreign policy during Monroe's time?

The Liberator

Document: William Lloyd Garrison, editorial in *The Liberator* (1831)

Historical Context

In 1835, a Boston mob almost hung William Lloyd Garrison. He was saved when the authorities put him in jail to protect him. This shows the excitement Garrison's ideas caused in Boston at that time. What were those ideas? Garrison was perhaps America's best-known abolitionist. Abolitionists wanted to abolish, or end, slavery. By the 1830s, Garrison had come to believe that slavery should end right away, without payment to slave owners for their losses.

Garrison was born in Newburyport, Massachusetts, in 1805. He was the son of a merchant sailor. As a teenager he worked for a Newburyport newspaper and later became its editor. Garrison began to oppose slavery as a young man. At first he favored helping freed slaves to settle in Africa. The American Colonization Society raised money to purchase slaves. The society encouraged the freed slaves to live in Liberia. This was a newly settled African colony (later a free nation) supported by the United States.

By 1830, Garrison came to believe that this approach was wrong. He thought it was too slow. He also thought that slave owners should not be paid to free their slaves. He was now working for an antislavery newspaper in Baltimore, Maryland. Quaker abolitionist Benjamin Lundy had started the paper, titled *The Genius of Universal Emancipation*. Then Garrison moved back north. On January 1, 1831, he began to publish his own Boston newspaper, *The Liberator*.

Of course, an immediate end to slavery was an unpopular idea in the slaveholding South. But it was also unpopular in the North when Garrison began to publish *The Liberator*. Different groups of Northerners opposed immediate abolition.

- For laborers, ending slavery threatened to increase competition for jobs. Freed slaves would be on an equal level with them.

- For the business class, the end of slavery threatened the peace between North and South. These people feared that business relationships might be upset. Northern factories manufactured textiles from Southern cotton.

- Many others may not have liked slavery, but they felt nothing was more important than a unified country. They feared that Garrison's ideas could cause a war between North and South.

The Liberator did not have a lot of readers. Most of the subscribers were African American. But Garrison became widely known as the spokesperson for a more radical form of abolition.

Importance

This 1831 editorial appeared in the first issue of *The Liberator*. It announces the newspaper's purpose and states Garrison's approach to ending slavery. He writes that slavery is moral issue, a question of right and wrong. To him, a person should not compromise with evil. When Garrison began his paper, his ideas were only accepted by a small group. In fact, his ideas angered most people. But Garrison did not give up. He later called the U.S. Constitution "a covenant with death and an agreement with Hell," because it permitted slavery. He then burned a copy of the Constitution. Garrison believed nothing was more important than ending slavery, even if it meant the nation coming apart. Although it took the Civil War to end slavery, many believe that Garrison's persistent voice had a part in that outcome.

William Lloyd Garrison, *The Liberator*, January 1, 1831

To the Public

. . . During my recent tour for the purpose of exciting the minds of the people by a series of discourses on the subject of slavery, every place that I visited gave fresh evidence of the fact, that a greater revolution in public sentiment was to be effected in the free states — and particularly in New-England — than at the south. I found contempt more bitter, opposition more active, detraction more relentless, prejudice more stubborn, and apathy more frozen, than among slave owners themselves. Of course, there were individual exceptions to the contrary. This state of things afflicted, but did not dishearten me. I determined, at every hazard, to lift up the standard of emancipation in the eyes of the nation, within sight of Bunker Hill and in the birth place of liberty. That standard is now unfurled; and long may it float, unhurt by the spoliations of time or the missiles of a desperate foe — yea, till every chain be broken, and every bondman set free! Let southern oppressors tremble — let their secret abettors tremble — let their northern apologists tremble — let all the enemies of the persecuted blacks tremble. . . .

Assenting to the "self-evident truth" maintained in the American Declaration of Independence, "that all men are created equal, and endowed by their Creator with certain inalienable rights — among which are life, liberty and the pursuit of happiness," I shall strenuously contend for the immediate enfranchisement of our slave population. In Park-street Church, on the Fourth of July, 1829, in an address on slavery, I

(continued)

unreflectingly assented to the popular but pernicious doctrine of gradual abolition. I seize this opportunity to make a full and unequivocal recantation, and thus publicly to ask pardon of my God, of my country, and of my brethren the poor slaves, for having uttered a sentiment so full of timidity, injustice and absurdity. A similar recantation, from my pen, was published in the Genius of Universal Emancipation at Baltimore, in September, 1829. My conscience is now satisfied.

I am aware, that many object to the severity of my language; but is there not cause for severity? I will be as harsh as truth, and as uncompromising as justice. On this subject, I do not wish to think, or speak, or write, with moderation. No! no! Tell a man whose house is on fire, to give a moderate alarm; tell him to moderately rescue his wife from the hand of the ravisher; tell the mother to gradually extricate her babe from the fire into which it has fallen; — but urge me not to use moderation in a cause like the present. I am in earnest — I will not equivocate — I will not excuse — I will not retreat a single inch — AND I WILL BE HEARD. The apathy of the people is enough to make every statue leap from its pedestal, and to hasten the resurrection of the dead. . . .

William Lloyd Garrison

Vocabulary

discourses—formal expressions of ideas on a subject

sentiment—feeling

contempt—the act of hating

detraction—the act of speaking badly about

relentless—steady, never giving up

apathy—lack of emotion, interest, or concern

afflicted—seriously upset

dishearten—to cause to lose spirit

hazard—danger

standard—a banner or emblem that is a rallying point for battle

emancipation—the act of freeing

spoliations—destructions

missiles—objects thrown

bondman—slave

abettors—people who assist

apologists—people who speak or write in defense of someone or something

persecuted—caused to suffer

self-evident truth—a fact that need not be proven

strenuously—energetically

enfranchisement—act of setting free

assented—agreed

pernicious—destructive

unequivocal—leaving no doubt

recantation—a public statement taking back something said previously

brethren—brothers

uttered—spoken

uncompromising—unyielding

moderation—the lessening of intensity

ravisher—rapist

extricate—to free or remove

earnest—a state of seriousness

equivocate—confuse or mislead

resurrection—bringing to life again

Comprehension Questions

1. To whom is the letter written?

2. What is the subject of the letter?

3. While he was speaking on his lecture tour, which part of the country did Garrison feel was most sympathetic to his views on slavery?

4. Where did he find the most opposition to his message?

5. What American document does he use to prove that slavery should be wrong in this country?

6. When does Garrison think slavery must end?

7. For what does he apologize?

8. What does Garrison insist that he will not do in his effort to end slavery?

Critical Thinking

1. What was the purpose of this editorial being included in the first issue of the newspaper?

2. What does Garrison mean when he says the "standard is now unfurled" and "long may it float" unharmed by a "desperate foe"? What is he comparing the newspaper to?

3. Why does Garrison think moderation is the wrong approach for ending slavery? What do you think of the comparisons he makes with other emergencies?

4. The last paragraph of this excerpt is the most famous of Garrison's words. Why do you think they are so often quoted?

5. If he were speaking these words, what would be Garrison's tone of voice?

Making Connections

1. When Garrison refers to slaves as "my brethren the poor slaves," what is he saying?

2. Why does Garrison use the words of the Declaration of Independence?

3. Garrison says he is aware that some people object to "the severity of my language." What is he referring to? Do you think the tone worked for him? What purpose did it serve?

4. Can you think of reform movements in American history that have stirred similar emotions as antislavery?

5. Garrison came to this view after having supported more gradual methods of ending slavery. Why do you think he changed?

6. What were the obstacles to immediate emancipation? Which of these were most serious?

Relating the Past to Our Lives

1. Garrison writes that he once held a view that he later changed. Can you think of some ideas you have had that have changed over time?

2. Are there social issues in today's society that have led to conflict similar to that over slavery? Explain.

3. When does compromising make sense and when is it not appropriate? Explain.

4. Have you ever taken a stand on an issue of importance to society? What did you do?

Essay Questions

1. Do you think Garrison's aggressive, uncompromising approach to ending slavery was the most effective approach? Why or why not?

2. Are there other methods that might be used to achieve Garrison's goals? What are their advantages and disadvantages?

3. Some historians have blamed abolitionists for increasing the conflict between North and South that led to the Civil War. Do you agree? Why or why not?

The Trail of Tears

Document: Letter from Chief John Ross to the U.S. Senate and House of Representatives (1836)

Historical Context

Without knowing what, the phrase "Trail of Tears" communicates something tragic. The event lives up to its name. It was the forced relocation at bayonet point of 16,000 Cherokee from their Georgia homes to Oklahoma. Along the way, 4,000 Cherokee died of cold, disease, and hunger.

White settlers began to move west beyond the Appalachian Mountains in the early 1800s. They found Indians "in the way." Many groups of Native Americans had long lived in the southeastern part of the United States. These native groups included Cherokee, Creek, Choctaw, Chickasaw, and Seminoles. They had lived a mostly undisturbed existence until white Americans began to overspread their lands. At first, these tribes resisted. Then they decided that they could best protect themselves by becoming farmers and slaveholders—by adopting the lifestyle of the settlers. Thereafter, these groups were called the Five Civilized Tribes. The Cherokee in Georgia made the most changes.

- They instituted a form of government with three branches.

- They developed a written language and published a newspaper in it.

- Many Cherokee took English names.

- Some owned slaves.

But these changes only postponed relocation. Georgia had always claimed control over Cherokee land. Then gold was discovered in the Georgia hills. In 1832, the Cherokee brought a case to the U.S. Supreme Court. The Court ruled that only the national government could deal with the Indians—not the states. Yet Georgia continued to enforce its laws on the Cherokee. President Andrew Jackson ignored the Court's ruling. Earlier, in 1830, Jackson had signed into law the Indian Removal Act. This law gave the president power to make treaties to remove Native Americans from their lands east of the Mississippi River in exchange for land west of the river.

The Cherokee government refused to sign a treaty to relocate, so the U.S. government resorted to a trick. In 1835, U.S. authorities convinced a small group of Cherokee to sign a relocation agreement called the Treaty of New Echota. It was signed without permission of the elected Cherokee government. By this treaty, the United States gave the Cherokee $5 million and paid for any buildings left behind. In return, the Cherokee were given land in Oklahoma. The U.S. Senate ratified the Treaty of New Echota by one vote. Chief John Ross insisted that the signers of the treaty did not represent the tribe. He circulated a petition signed by more than 15,000 Cherokee opposing the treaty. Congress did not reconsider. The

Cherokee nation protested the treaty until 1838. At that time President Martin Van Buren sent the army to forcibly remove the Cherokee. Under army guard, the Cherokee nation marched to Indian Country—Oklahoma.

Importance

This letter sent to Congress asks its members to reconsider its recognition of the Treaty of New Echota. Ross uses language he hopes Congress will understand. It is the language the Cherokee used when they adopted their U.S.-style form of government—the language of individual rights and fairness. A tone of desperation fills the letter. This reflects the Cherokee's anxiety about having to make a new life in an environment they had never seen. It is an excellent source for understanding the loss of Indian land from the Native Americans' point of view.

Letter from Chief John Ross, "To the Senate and House of Representatives," September 28, 1836

It is well known that for a number of years past we have been harassed by a series of vexations, which it is deemed unnecessary to recite in detail, but the evidence of which our delegation will be prepared to furnish. With a view to bringing our troubles to a close, a delegation was appointed on the 23rd of October, 1835, by the General Council of the nation, clothed with full powers to enter into arrangements with the Government of the United States, for the final adjustment of all our existing difficulties. The delegation failing to effect an arrangement with the United States commissioner, then in the nation, proceeded, agreeably to their instructions in that case, to Washington City, for the purpose of negotiating a treaty with the authorities of the United States.

After the departure of the Delegation, a contract was made by the Rev. John F. Schermerhorn, and certain individual Cherokees, purporting to be a "treaty, concluded at New Echota, in the State of Georgia, on the 29th day of December, 1835, by General William Carroll and John F. Schermerhorn, commissioners on the part of the United States, and the chiefs, headmen, and people of the Cherokee tribes of Indians." A spurious Delegation, in violation of a special injunction of the general council of the nation, proceeded to Washington City with this pretended treaty, and by false and fraudulent representations supplanted in the favor of the Government the legal and accredited Delegation of the Cherokee

(continued)

people, and obtained for this instrument, after making important alterations in its provisions, the recognition of the United States Government. And now it is presented to us as a treaty, ratified by the Senate, and approved by the President, and our acquiescence in its requirements demanded, under the sanction of the displeasure of the United States, and the threat of summary compulsion, in case of refusal. . . .

By the stipulations of this instrument, we are despoiled of our private possessions, the indefeasible property of individuals. We are stripped of every attribute of freedom and eligibility for legal self-defence. Our property may be plundered before our eyes; violence may be committed on our persons; even our lives may be taken away, and there is none to regard our complaints. We are denationalized; we are disfranchised. We are deprived of membership in the human family! We have neither land nor home, nor resting place that can be called our own. And this is effected by the provisions of a compact which assumes the venerated, the sacred appellation of treaty.

We are overwhelmed! Our hearts are sickened, our utterance is paralyzed, when we reflect on the condition in which we are placed, by the audacious practices of unprincipled men, who have managed their stratagems with so much dexterity as to impose on the Government of the United States, in the face of our earnest, solemn, and reiterated protestations.

The instrument in question is not the act of our Nation; we are not parties to its covenants; it has not received the sanction of our people. The makers of it sustain no office nor appointment in our Nation, under the designation of Chiefs, Head men, or any other title, by which they hold, or could acquire, authority to assume the reins of Government, and to make bargain and sale of our rights, our possessions, and our common country. And we are constrained solemnly to declare, that we cannot but contemplate the enforcement of the stipulations of this instrument on us, against our consent, as an act of injustice and oppression, which, we are well persuaded, can never knowingly be countenanced by the Government and people of the United States; nor can we believe it to be the design of these honorable and highminded individuals, who stand at the head of the Govt., to bind a whole Nation, by the acts of a few unauthorized individuals. And, therefore, we, the parties to be affected by the result, appeal with confidence to the justice, the magnanimity, the compassion, of your honorable bodies, against the enforcement, on us, of the provisions of a compact, in the formation of which we have had no agency.

From *The Papers of Chief John Ross, 1807–1839, Volume I*, edited by Gary Moulton, University of Oklahoma Press, 1985.

Vocabulary

harassed—repeatedly bothered

vexations—annoyances, troubles

deemed—considered

recite—to say

delegation—group of representatives

authorities—people in position of responsibility

departure—act of leaving

spurious—not legitimate

injunction—order

fraudulent—illegal

supplanted—replaced

accredited—officially recognized

alterations—changes

acquiescence—the act of quietly accepting

sanction—authorized enforcement

summary compulsion—something made to happen without delay

stipulations—parts of an agreement

despoiled—stripped

indefeasible—not capable of being undone

attribute—characteristic

plundered—taken by force

denationalized—stripped of membership in a nation

disfranchised—stripped of rights

compact—agreement

venerated—respected

sacred appellation—very respected name

paralyzed—powerless

audacious—bold

stratagems—schemes, tricks

dexterity—skill

impose—to force upon

reiterated—repeatedly voiced

covenants—agreements

sanction—approval

sustain—to hold

designation—title

reins—controlling power

constrained—forced

contemplate—to consider

instrument—legal document

countenanced—approved of

magnanimity—generosity

compassion—sympathy for another's pain

agency—the act of exerting power

Comprehension Questions

1. What position does the writer hold among the Cherokee?

2. Who is the intended audience of this letter?

3. What had the Cherokee nation done to solve the problems they had over land?

4. After the Cherokee representatives failed to reach an agreement, how was a treaty made? What was the treaty called?

5. What did Ross write about those who represented the Cherokee at New Echota?

6. How did the U.S. government respond to the Treaty of New Echota?

7. According to Ross, what does the treaty mean for the Cherokee?

8. How does Ross say the Cherokee feel about their situation?

9. What does Ross say is the opinion of the Cherokee nation about the Treaty of New Echota?

10. What does Ross ask Congress to do?

Critical Thinking

1. What sentence best sums up the main idea of this letter?

2. Do you think Ross is accurate concerning the way the treaty was made? Do you think the Senate knows it?

3. Do you think Ross has a chance of convincing the Senate?

4. What is the tone of Ross's letter?

5. Evaluate the steps Ross took to convince Congress of his position.

Making Connections

1. List a couple of the "vexations" that the Cherokee experienced before the Treaty of New Echota.

2. Why is the U.S. government trying to move all Native Americans west of the Mississippi River?

3. On a U.S. map, compute the approximate number of miles from western Georgia to Oklahoma. How long would it take to walk this distance at two miles per hour?

Relating the Past to Our Lives

1. What would you have done if you were a Cherokee in Georgia at the time?

2. Can you think of any recent events when one group forced another group of people to move from their homes? Explain.

3. Do you think this could happen in the United States today? Explain.

Essay Questions

1. Ross wrote that the delegation that signed the treaty did so "in violation of a special injunction of the general council of the nation." This refers to a Cherokee law that punished with death any Cherokee who sold land to the U.S. government. Why would the Cherokee pass such a law? What do you think of this law?

2. President Jackson said that he was moving Native Americans to the West for their own good. To what extent is that true? To what extent is that false?

3. John Ross and most of the Cherokee nation refused to comply with the Treaty of New Echota. In return, the U.S. government did not give the Cherokee the $5 million promised to them in the treaty and forced them to move anyway. Did Ross make a bad decision? Explain your answer.

The Lowell Mills

Document: "The Spirit of Discontent," fictional piece published in the *Lowell Offering* (1840)

Historical Context

What would convince a New England farmer of the 1820s and 1830s to send his teenage daughter to a city to work in a factory? This is the question the mill owners in Lowell, Massachusetts, needed to answer. They needed workers for these early textile factories. This was before large numbers of poor immigrants came to the United States looking for work. New England's economy was still based on farming. Sons were essential to their family's economy. This left daughters. If they worked outside the farm, they could also add to the family income.

But the mill owners in Lowell, Massachusetts, understood the image mill towns had in many American minds. When Americans thought about factories, British mill towns such as Birmingham and Manchester came to mind. These were notorious for dirty, unsafe conditions. These cities quickly became run down. Polluted rivers caused disease. Smoke darkened the sky. Workers labored long hours in unsafe conditions for low wages. Sadly, children as young as nine or ten were among these workers.

Lowell mill owners wanted to change this image. They decided to create a different kind of mill town in order to attract female workers from New England farms. They planned Lowell with these young women in mind.

- Along with brick factories, space was set aside for flower gardens and trees.

- Near the factory buildings, dormitories were built to house the girls. An older woman supervised the girls in each dormitory.

- Stores of every type were built.

- Opportunities for enrichment were provided. The factory girls could spend their free time at lectures or courses to improve their minds.

- Many churches were available for the factory girls' moral instruction.

For many young women, life at Lowell offered opportunities and an independence unavailable on the farm. Yet, the work did involve long hours. It was increasingly dull and sometimes dangerous. In time, competition from other factories caused the owners to increase the girls' workload. Some young women were so discontented that in 1845 they organized to improve conditions. They attempted to limit their hours to ten per day. But they were unsuccessful. By the late 1840s and 1850s, large numbers of Irish immigrants began to replace the girls by working for lower wages. In many ways, Lowell became a typical mill town over time. The experiment was over.

Importance

This dialogue is taken from the *Lowell Offering*, a literary magazine written and published by the factory girls. They were the audience. The dialogue was published in 1840 by a girl who calls herself Almira. In the conversation, Almira and another female factory worker discuss the advantages and disadvantages for girls who choose to live and work in Lowell. While fictional, the dialogue no doubt raises issues that at least some factory girls discussed. The selection helps the reader understand the life at Lowell.

Anonymous, "The Spirit of Discontent," 1840

"I will not stay in Lowell any longer; I am determined to give my notice this very day," said Ellen Collins, as the earliest bell was tolling to remind us of the hour for labor.

"Why, what is the matter, Ellen? It seems to me you have dreamed out a new idea! Where do you think of going? and what for?"

"I am going home, where I shall not be obliged to rise so early in the morning, nor be dragged about by the ringing of a bell, nor confined in a close noisy room from morning till night. I will not stay here; I am determined to go home in a fortnight."

Such was our brief morning's conversation.

In the evening, as I sat alone, reading, my companions having gone out to public lectures or social meetings, Ellen entered. . . .

"And so, Ellen," said I, "you think it unpleasant to rise so early in the morning, and be confined in the noisy mill so many hours during the day. And I think so, too. All this, and much more, is very annoying, no doubt. But we must not forget that there are advantages, as well as disadvantages, in this employment, as in every other. If we expect to find all sun-shine and flowers in any station in life, we shall most surely be disappointed. We are very busily engaged during the day; but then we have the evening to ourselves, with no one to dictate to or control us. I have frequently heard you say, that you would not be confined to house-hold duties, and that you disliked the millinery business altogether, because you could not have your evenings, for leisure. You know that in Lowell we have schools, lectures, and meetings of every description, for moral and intellectual improvement."

(continued)

"All that is very true," replied Ellen, "but if we were to attend every public institution, and every evening school which offers itself for our improvement, we might spend every farthing of our earnings, and even more. Then if sickness should overtake us, what are the probable consequences? Here we are, far from kindred and home; and if we have an empty purse, we shall be destitute of *friends* also."

"I do not think so, Ellen. I believe there is no place where there are so many advantages within the reach of the laboring class of people, as exist here; where there is so much equality, so few aristocratic distinctions, and such good fellowship, as may be found in this community. A person has only to be honest, industrious, and moral, to secure the respect of the virtuous and good, though he may not be worth a dollar; while on the other hand, an immoral person, though he should possess wealth, is not respected."

"As to the morality of the place," returned Ellen, "I have no fault to find. I object to the constant hurry of every thing. We cannot have time to eat, drink or sleep; we have only thirty minutes, or at most three quarters of an hour, allowed us, to go from our work, partake of our food, and return to the noisy clatter of machinery. Up before day, at the clang of the bell—and out of the mill by the clang of the bell—into the mill, and at work, in obedience to that ding-dong of a bell—just as though we were so many living machines. I will give my notice to-morrow: go, I will—I won't stay here and be a white slave." . . .

I saw that my discontented friend was not in a humour to give me an answer—and I therefore went on with my talk.

"You are fully aware, Ellen, that a country life does not exclude people from labor—to say nothing of the inferior privileges of attending public worship—that people have often to go a distance to meeting of any kind—that books cannot be so easily obtained as they can here—that you cannot always have just such society as you wish—that you"—

She interrupted me, by saying, "We have no bell, with its everlasting ding-dong."

"What difference does it make," said I, "whether you shall be awaked by a bell, or the noisy bustle of a farm-house? For, you know, farmers are generally up as early in the morning as we are obliged to rise."

(continued)

 www.socialstudies.com/walch

"But then," said Ellen, "country people have none of the clattering of machinery constantly dinning in their ears."

"True," I replied, "but they have what is worse—and that is, a dull, lifeless silence all around them. The hens may cackle sometimes, and the geese gabble, and the pigs squeal"—

Ellen's hearty laugh interrupted my description—and presently we proceeded very pleasantly, to compare a country life with a factory life in Lowell. Her scowl of discontent had departed, and she was prepared to consider the subject candidly. We agreed, that since we must work for a living, the mill, all things considered, is the most pleasant, and best calculated to promote our welfare; that we will work diligently during the hours of labor; improve our leisure to the best advantage, in the cultivation of the mind, —hoping thereby not only to increase our own pleasure, but also to add to the happiness of those around us.

ALMIRA

Vocabulary

tolling—ringing

obliged—required

fortnight—two weeks

confined—kept indoors

station—position

dictate to—order

millinery business—women's hat-making business

farthing—a British coin of low value

destitute—lacking something needed or desirable

aristocratic distinctions—social-class divisions

fellowship—companionship

industrious—hardworking

clatter—rattling sound

inferior—of poor quality

bustle—activity

 www.socialstudies.com/walch

dinning—making a loud continued noise

candidly—honestly

calculated—designed

welfare—well-being

diligently—with a steady, earnest, and energetic effort

cultivation—improvement

Comprehension Questions

1. What has Ellen decided to do?

2. How does the author respond?

3. What does Ellen dislike about her work conditions?

4. How does the author reply to this complaint?

5. What advantage does the author say the factory job has over working elsewhere?

6. How does Ellen respond to the suggestion that Lowell offers advantages for learning?

7. What does the author say about Lowell regarding equality?

8. What are Ellen's objections to the factory schedule?

9. How does the author answer Ellen's objection to the factory bell?

10. How does the author respond to Ellen's objection to the noise of the machines?

11. What did Almira and Ellen finally agree on?

12. *Note:* As an alternative to questions 3–10, students might list the points made in the discussion in two columns entitled "Advantages" and "Disadvantages."

Critical Thinking

1. Are some of the advantages or disadvantages discussed by Almira and Ellen more important than others? Explain.

2. Why do you think the author wrote the dialogue?

3. Why do you think the author chose this subject to write about?

4. Do you think the independence and learning opportunities Lowell offered outweighed the difficulty of factory work?

5. Do you think the mill owners would be pleased with this piece of fiction? Explain.

Making Connections

1. The story is fictional. Do you think it accurately represents issues the young women working at the mills discuss? Explain.

2. Why do you think the author wrote this as a conversation?

3. Do you think the factory girls wanted to spend a large part of their lives working at the mills? Explain.

4. How did working in a factory fit with the image of a young lady's role in society? Explain.

Relating the Past to Our Lives

1. Many of the mill girls were your age. How would you feel about being away from your parents without e-mail, telephone, or a fast way to return home to visit?

2. When someone works, a trade is made between the work and its reward. Do you have a job? Is the reward worth it? Explain.

3. When you have an important decision to make, to whom do you turn for advice? How much influence does that person have with you?

Essay Questions

1. Using the information in the conversation, write a diary entry for a Lowell mill girl describing a typical day. You can emphasize the advantages or disadvantages or try to balance them.

2. Was the Lowell mill system an advance for women? Explain.

3. Were the owners of the mills most interested in the welfare of the girls in the mills, or in making a profit? Explain.

Conditions for the Mentally Ill

Document: Dorothea Dix, "Memorial to the Massachusetts Legislature" (1843)

Historical Context

"The insane do not feel heat or cold," officials responded to Dorothea Dix. She had asked them why conditions for the mentally ill in the East Cambridge (Massachusetts) jail were so miserable. Dix had been invited to teach female inmates at the prison. After observing the way "the insane" were housed, Dix found a new direction.

Dorothea Lynde Dix was born in 1802 in Hampden, Maine, still a part of Massachusetts at the time. From the age of fourteen, Dix taught school. But her experience in that jail in 1841 led her to begin a crusade that would occupy many of the following years.

State policy was to house mentally ill people with criminals in prison or with the poor in almshouses. At the time, most Americans believed the "insane" could not be cured. Therefore, keeping them in convenient, inexpensive holding areas could not affect them negatively. Dix disagreed. She believed the mental health of mentally ill people could improve. She also felt that humane living conditions might help in recovery. There did exist a few humane institutions for the mentally ill. But these were rare—and usually reserved for the wealthy. Most mentally ill people were left unclothed in the dark, without heat, often chained to walls in jails and poorhouses. Dix wanted to change that.

With notebook in hand, she traveled the state jotting down conditions she saw in jails and poorhouses. Two years later, in 1843, she wrote her memorial to the Massachusetts legislature. A memorial is a statement of fact addressed to a government, often in the form of a petition. Samuel Gridley Howe, director of the Perkins School for the Blind, delivered the memorial.

Dix's words led directly to change. After some debate, the legislature voted to expand the Worcester state hospital for the insane. But Dix did not stop in Massachusetts. She traveled 30,000 miles in three years to address lawmakers in other states. Her work led directly to the founding of thirty-two mental hospitals. At the time she began, only thirteen existed in the entire country.

Importance

This document is important because it represents the reform spirit that developed in the 1830s and 1840s. Many movements arose that intended to improve American society. Abolitionism, temperance, prison reform, world peace, communes, education reform, and vegetarianism were just some of these. A few factors led to this.

- Populations in the cities were growing, bringing people in closer contact with each other. Social problems became more obvious.

- Evangelical religion became popular. Many believed anyone, no matter how immoral, could recognize his or her sins and live a holy life. This positive outlook led many to believe society could also be saved.

- The United States was a young nation beginning to develop. Many reformers seized the opportunity to make an American society without the problems of European societies.

Many reformers were women. But they rarely took a leadership role as Dix did. A woman's role in society was clearly defined—home, children, and morality. Public life was not a place for women. But social reform as an extension of the home became the exception. Social reforms dealt with morality and so were in women's realm. Also, many social problems such as excessive drinking and crime affected the home, also women's realm.

Dorothea Dix, Memorial to the Massachusetts Legislature, 1843

Gentlemen, —I respectfully ask to present this Memorial . . .

About two years since leisure afforded opportunity and duty prompted me to visit several prisons and almshouses in the vicinity of this metropolis. I found, near Boston, in the jails and asylums for the poor, a numerous class brought into unsuitable connection with criminals and the general mass of paupers. I refer to idiots and insane persons, dwelling in circumstances not only adverse to their own physical and moral improvement, but productive of extreme disadvantages to all other persons brought into association with them. . . . I shall be obliged to speak with great plainness, and to reveal many things revolting to the taste, and from which my woman's nature shrinks with peculiar sensitiveness. But truth is the highest consideration. I tell what I have seen—painful and shocking as the details often are—that from them you may feel more deeply the imperative obligation which lies upon you to prevent the possibility of a repetition or continuance of such outrages upon humanity. . . .

I must confine myself to few examples, but am ready to furnish other and more complete details, if required. . . .

(continued)

I proceed, gentlemen, briefly to call your attention to the present state of insane persons confined within this Commonwealth, in cages, closets, cellars, stalls, pens! Chained, naked, beaten with rods, and lashed into obedience. . . .

I repeat it, it is defective legislation which perpetuates and multiplies these abuses. In illustration of my subject, I offer the following extracts from my Note-book and Journal: —

Lincoln. A woman in a cage. Medford. One idiotic subject chained, and one in a close stall for seventeen years. Pepperell. One often doubly chained, hand and foot; another violent; several peaceable now. Brookfield. One man caged, comfortable. Granville. One often closely confined; now losing the use of his limbs from want of exercise. . . .

Dedham. The insane disadvantageously placed in the jail. In the almshouse, two females in stalls, situated in the main building; lie in wooden bunks filled with straw; always shut up. One of these subjects is supposed curable. The overseers of the poor have declined giving her a trial at the hospital, as I was informed, on account of expense. . . .

Men of Massachusetts, I beg, I implore . . .

Become the benefactors of your race, the just guardians of the solemn rights you hold in trust. Raise up the fallen, succor the desolate, restore the outcast, defend the helpless, and for your eternal and great reward receive the benediction, "Well done, good and faithful servants, become rulers over many things!"

Injustice is also done to the convicts: it is certainly very wrong that they should be doomed day after day and night after night to listen to the ravings of madmen and madwomen. This is a kind of punishment that is not recognized by our statutes, and is what the criminal ought not to be called upon to undergo. . . .

Gentlemen, I commit to you this sacred cause. Your action upon this subject will affect the present and future condition of hundreds and of thousands. In this legislation, as in all things, may you exercise that "wisdom which is the breath of the power of God." Respectfully Submitted, D. L. Dix

Vocabulary

memorial—statement of facts addressed to a government

afforded—made available

prompted—moved to action

almshouses—poorhouses, places for poor people maintained at public expense

vicinity—surrounding area

metropolis—city

asylums—institutions for care of sick or poor people

unsuitable—not appropriate

paupers—poor people

idiots—term used at the time for people with severe mental retardation

dwelling—living

adverse to—against

association—being together with

obliged—required

revolting—disgusting

nature—basic makeup

imperative obligation—something that must be done

confine—to restrict

furnish—to provide

defective legislation—bad law

perpetuates—continues

illustration—example

extracts—selections

limbs—arms and legs

disadvantageously—unfavorably

situated—located

overseers—supervisors

implore—to beg urgently

benefactors—people who cause positive things

guardians—ones responsible for care of others

solemn—serious

succor—aid

desolate—lonely

outcast—person rejected by society

benediction—giving of a blessing

statutes—laws

undergo—to endure

commit—to entrust

sacred—worthy

Comprehension Questions

1. Who is Dix's intended audience?

2. What institutions did Dix report visiting during the past two years? in what geographical area?

3. What groups did Dix find housed together in these places?

4. What is Dix's opinion of what she will describe? Why does she report these observations in spite of this?

5. In what places did Dix find mentally ill people being held?

6. Who does Dix believe deserves blame for these conditions?

7. List three towns Dix visited in her survey of living conditions for mentally ill people.

8. What does Dix ask the lawmakers to do?

9. What other groups are suffering due to being housed with mentally ill people?

Critical Thinking

1. What is the main idea of Dix's memorial?

2. What makes Dix's description of conditions in the poorhouse and jail believable?

3. What would Dix consider a successful result of her work?

4. Does Dix organize her argument well? What do you like about it?

5. Was Dix's audience appropriate for her purpose, or should she have tried addressing a different audience?

Making Connections

1. Who might be angered by Dix's memorial?

2. Why do you think mentally ill people were being housed in the way Dix discovered?

3. Women played a large part in many nineteenth-century reform movements. Why do you think that was?

4. Why was speaking for the welfare of mentally ill people unusual at the time?

5. How might Dix's experience as a teacher have influenced her to work for mentally ill people?

6. Dix did not read her memorial to the Massachusetts legislature. Samuel Gridley Howe did instead. Why you think that was?

Relating the Past to Our Lives

1. Have you ever signed a petition to a legislature? Explain. Do you think petitions to legislatures are effective?

2. This was a case where a single individual effected change. She was the entire movement in the beginning. Can you think of an instance when that has happened today?

3. Compare what Dix described with the treatment of mentally ill people today.

Essay Questions

1. Were reforms such as improved care for mentally ill people, women's rights, temperance, and abolitionism consistent with the spirit of the Age of Democracy of the 1830s? Explain.

2. Compare the message, audience, and tone of Dix's memorial with William Lloyd Garrison's editorial in *The Liberator*. How are they similar? How are they different? Why did Dix's memorial have such an immediate effect?

3. Do you think other reformers, such as those who wanted to end slavery, improve education, and increase the rights of women, would agree with Dix's goal?

The Mexican War

Document: James K. Polk, message to Congress (May 11, 1846)

Historical Context

What is a sufficient reason to go to war? This question remains as critical today as in the past. In 1846, the disputed reasons for the onset of the Mexican War caused division among Americans. The war's outcome in 1848 was the acquisition of the American Southwest and California. This outcome became the war's justification for many Americans.

Wars often have long-term and short-term causes or trigger points. Among the long-term causes of the Mexican War were these:

- An expansionist urge existed among U.S. policy makers. They used the idea of Manifest Destiny to justify expansion. According to Manifest Destiny, it was God's will for the United States to expand westward across the entire continent.

- Mexico was angry over Texas joining the United States in 1845. Earlier, the Mexican government had invited Americans to settle in Texas, then a province of Mexico. Settlers only needed to become Mexican citizens and follow Mexican law to acquire land. But the Texans eventually fought a war of independence against Mexico. Texas won and became its own country in 1836. The Mexican government believed that the U.S. government had backed the independence effort. To avoid war with Mexico, the United States turned down Texans' request for their republic to become a U.S. state. In 1845, though, the United States changed its policy and annexed Texas.

- The United States wanted the ports and resources of the West. Ports on the Pacific Ocean would provide easier access to the China trade.

- Northerners suspected that Southerners wanted the war because, like Texas, Mexican lands might produce slave states.

- Americans living in Mexico had suffered loss of property and injuries during various Mexican revolutions. The Mexican government had not settled claims for payment for those losses.

When James K. Polk ran for president in 1845, he promised to expand the country's borders. When Texas was admitted to the Union in 1845, Mexico broke off diplomatic relations with the United States. Disagreement over the southern border of Texas followed. The historical border of the Mexican state of Texas had been the Nueces River. Congressman Abraham Lincoln agreed with Mexico on the Nueces River as the boundary. However, the United States claimed the border was the Rio Grande. (Polk called this river the Rio del Norte in his message to Congress.) The Rio Grande was farther south than the Nueces. Using it as a border for Texas gave the United States more land.

Polk sent James Slidell to Mexico to negotiate the border. He also gave Slidell authority to offer up to $30 million for the Mexican provinces of New Mexico and California. The Mexican government refused to meet with Slidell. In the meantime, Polk sent troops under General Zachary Taylor to occupy the disputed land between the Nueces and Rio Grande. Ulysses S. Grant was with Taylor. He wrote in a letter that the U.S. troops were sent to provoke an attack—to create a reason to go to war. Meanwhile, Polk was writing a war message to Congress. He claimed in the message that in refusing to see Slidell, Mexico had gravely insulted the United States. Before the message could be delivered, the trigger point happened—literally. Taylor ignored a warning that his troops occupied Mexican land. Mexican troops then fired on the Americans.

Importance

The U.S. Constitution requires a president to ask Congress for a war declaration by majority vote of both houses. The last officially declared U.S. war was World War II. When a president makes an argument for war, he focuses on the facts and interpretations he wants Congress to hear. Bear this in mind as you are reading Polk's message to Congress.

James K. Polk, Message to Congress, May 11, 1846

Washington, May 11, 1846

To the Senate and House of Representatives:

The existing state of the relations between the United States and Mexico renders it proper that I should bring the subject to the consideration of Congress. . . .

The strong desire to establish peace with Mexico on liberal and honorable terms, and the readiness of this Government to regulate and adjust our boundary and other causes of difference with that power on such fair and equitable principles as would lead to permanent relations of the most friendly nature, induced me in September last to seek the reopening of diplomatic relations between the two countries. . . . An envoy of the United States repaired to Mexico with full powers to adjust every existing difference. But though present on the Mexican soil by agreement between the two Governments, invested with full powers, and bearing evidence of the most friendly dispositions, his mission has been unavailing. The Mexican Government not only refused to receive him or listen to his propositions, but after a long-continued series of menaces have at last invaded our territory and shed the blood of our fellow-citizens on our own soil. . . .

(continued)

In my message at the commencement of the present session I informed you that upon the earnest appeal both of the Congress and convention of Texas I had ordered an efficient military force to take a position between the Nueces and the Del Norte. This had become necessary to meet a threatened invasion of Texas by the Mexican forces, for which extensive military preparations had been made. The invasion was threatened solely because Texas had determined, in accordance with a solemn resolution of the Congress of the United States, to annex herself to our Union, and under these circumstances it was plainly our duty to extend our protection over her citizens and soil. . . .

The Congress of Texas, by its act of December 19, 1836, had declared the Rio del Norte to be the boundary of that Republic. Its jurisdiction had been extended and exercised beyond the Nueces. The country between that river and the Del Norte had been represented in the Congress and in the convention of Texas, had thus taken part in the act of annexation itself, and is now included within one of our Congressional districts. Our own Congress had, moreover, with great unanimity, by the act approved December 31, 1845, recognized the country beyond the Nueces as a part of our territory by including it within our own revenue system, and a revenue officer to reside within that district has been appointed by and with the advice and consent of the Senate. It became, therefore, of urgent necessity to provide for the defense of that portion of our country. Accordingly, on the 13th of January last instructions were issued to the general in command of these troops to occupy the left bank of the Del Norte. This river, which is the southwestern boundary of the State of Texas, is an exposed frontier. . . .

The Mexican forces at Matamoras assumed a belligerent attitude, and on the 12th of April General Ampudia, then in command, notified General Taylor to break up his camp within twenty-four hours and to retire beyond the Nueces River, and in the event of his failure to comply with these demands announced that arms, and arms alone, must decide the question. But no open act of hostility was committed until the 14th of April. On that day General Arista, who had succeeded to the command of the Mexican forces, communicated to General Taylor that he considered hostilities commenced and should prosecute them. A party of dragoons of 63 men and officers were on the same day dispatched from the American camp up the Rio del Norte, on its left bank, to ascertain whether the Mexican troops had crossed or were preparing to cross the

(continued)

river, became engaged with a large body of these troops, and after a short affair, in which some 16 were killed and wounded, appear to have been surrounded and compelled to surrender. . . .

[A]fter reiterated menaces, Mexico has passed the boundary of the United States, has invaded our territory and shed American blood upon the American soil. . . .

As war exists, and, notwithstanding all our efforts to avoid it, exists by the act of Mexico herself, we are called upon by every consideration of duty and patriotism to vindicate with decision the honor, the rights, and the interests of our country. . . .

In making these recommendations I deem it proper to declare that it is my anxious desire not only to terminate hostilities speedily, but to bring all matters in dispute between this Government and Mexico to an early and amicable adjustment; and in this view I shall be prepared to renew negotiations whenever Mexico shall be ready to receive propositions or to make propositions of her own. . . .

James K. Polk

Vocabulary

renders—makes

regulate—to control

equitable—on an equal basis

induced—persuaded

envoy—a representative of a government sent to a foreign country

repaired—went

invested—granted authority

dispositions—attitudes

unavailing—useless

propositions—ideas

menaces—threats

commencement—beginning

earnest—serious

convention—assembly of delegates

solemn—serious

resolution—formal expression of opinion

annex—to join

jurisdiction—authority

unanimity—the state of having the agreement of all parties

revenue system—tax system

consent—permission

portion—part

exposed—unprotected

belligerent—warlike

comply with—obey

hostility—acts of war

committed—made

commenced—begun

prosecute—follow to the end

dragoons—mounted troops

ascertain—to figure out

compelled—forced

reiterated—repeated

notwithstanding—despite

vindicate—to defend and uphold

deem—to consider

terminate—to end

amicable—friendly

renew—to begin again

propositions—things offered for consideration

Comprehension Questions

1. Who is the audience for this message?

2. What step does Polk say he took to preserve peace between Mexico and the United States?

3. How did Mexico respond to this?

4. According to Polk, what military actions did Mexico then take?

5. Where had Polk placed American troops?

6. Why does Polk say that Mexico threatened to invade the United States?

7. When Texas became an independent republic, what did it claim as its southern boundary?

8. How did the Mexican army respond to American troops stationed between the Nueces and Del Norte?

9. How many soldiers were killed eventually?

10. Who is to blame for the war, according to Polk?

Critical Thinking

1. Why does Polk include a description of his diplomatic efforts?

2. Polk argues for the Rio del Norte as the southern boundary of Texas. Why do you think that is?

3. The Mexican government disagreed on the boundary, believing it was the Nueces River. How do you think that figured in the Mexican decision to attack?

4. According to Polk, what part did the U.S. government play in starting the war? Is this accurate? Why or why not?

5. How reliable is a speech asking for a war declaration in giving a fair description of the positions of both sides? Why?

6. List the reasons Polk offers for problems between the United States and Mexico before troops were fired upon. Which is the most serious? Which is the easiest to settle in a friendly way?

Making Connections

1. Why is Polk sending this message to Congress?

2. Why would Mexico be angry with the U.S. government over Texas joining the United States?

3. Many Americans at the time disagreed with fighting the Mexican War. Why do you think this was?

4. Use a map to locate the disputed southern boundary between Texas and Mexico. Be sure to look for the Rio Grande rather than the Rio del Norte.

5. What other wars in U.S. history have caused controversy? Why?

Relating the Past to Our Lives

1. If you were a member of Congress in 1846, would you have voted for war with Mexico? Explain your answer.

2. How do you think Mexican textbooks today interpret the Mexican War?

3. The American Southwest gained as a result of the war contains large numbers of Mexican immigrants today. Why do you think Mexicans come to the United States today both legally and illegally?

Essay Questions

1. Who was most to blame for the war, Mexico or the United States? Discuss the parts each side played in the war's outbreak.

2. Did the United States want the Mexican War? Explain your answer.

3. The Mexican land gained as a result of the war had both immediate and long-term influences on the United States. Explain at least one of each.

The California Gold Rush

Document: Luzena Stanley Wilson, forty-niner; memories recalled in 1881 for her daughter Correnah Wilson Wright

Historical Context

Imagine walking from Missouri to California. What would make someone want to do this? Visions of free, fertile land and a better life brought many settlers west to Oregon in the 1840s. California settlers had migrated in smaller numbers. Until 1848, California was Mexican territory. But in 1849, thousands of settlers headed to California with a greater sense of urgency. Why? Gold had been discovered at Sutter's Mill near Sacramento. James Sutter was a rancher with visions of a cattle empire. He had hired James Marshall to build a sawmill on the American River. In January 1848, Marshall fished a lump of gold from the river. Soon word spread to the East. During 1849, scores of fortune seekers left their former lives behind, packed what they could carry, and headed west. They were called forty-niners. By the end of 1849, 80,000 fortune seekers had arrived in California.

Travelers to California went by one of three routes, each with advantages and disadvantages.

- The route by ship went south from eastern ports, around South America's Cape Horn, and then north to San Francisco. The trip could take six months, at a cost of $150 to $200 per passenger. Many passengers suffered seasickness along the way. But people from the East with some money found this to be the best route.

- A faster route combined sea and land. Travelers left the East Coast by ship, arriving at today's Panama. This was the shortest stretch of land between the Caribbean Sea and the Pacific Ocean. Passengers walked the fifty miles to the Pacific. Malaria and thieves along the way were among the hazards. If the fortune seekers survived those hardships, they had to wait on the western coast for another ship to carry them north to California. The wait was unpredictable. It could be weeks—or months.

- The route used by most was the overland 2,000-mile Oregon-California Trail. This was the best alternative for travelers in the middle part of the county or those in the East with limited funds. The travel pace was the speed at which horses, oxen, and people walk. Hostile Indians always presented a concern, as did snow in the mountains. But water was the biggest problem. Along the way, settlers who thought ahead sold extra water to those who had not for $100 per glass.

Although the earliest arrivals found gold worth millions, it dried up by mid-1849. Most forty-niners found no gold left to pan in rivers. Some left California. Most, though, stayed to pursue business chances that the booming population and abundance of money presented. The sudden growth of San Francisco led to a need for merchants, lawyers, doctors, hotels, and more. Luzena Wilson and her husband and two children traveled from

Missouri along the overland route. The family settled in Sacramento 1849, where they kept a hotel.

Importance

Luzena Wilson's book is a firsthand account dictated to her daughter in 1881. It offers an excellent window into the feelings of a woman making a life-changing, difficult journey. Keep in mind that it is a recollection thirty-two years later recorded by someone else. Memory is selective, and recollections are not the same as diaries.

Luzena Stanley Wilson, forty-niner, memories recalled in 1881 for her daughter Correnah Wilson Wright

The gold excitement spread like wildfire, even out to our log cabin in the prairie, and as we had almost nothing to lose, and we might gain a fortune, we early caught the fever. My husband grew enthusiastic and wanted to start immediately, but I would not be left behind. I thought where he could go I could, and where I went I could take my two little toddling babies. Mother-like, my first thought was of my children. I little realized then the task I had undertaken. If I had, I think I should still be in my log cabin in Missouri. But when we talked it all over, it sounded like such a small task to go out to California, and once there fortune, of course, would come to us. . . .

Monday we were to be off. Saturday we looked over our belongings, and threw aside what was not absolutely necessary. Beds we must have, and something to eat. It was a strange but comprehensive load which we stowed away in our "prairie-schooner," and some things which I thought necessities when we started became burdensome luxuries, and before many days I dropped by the road-side a good many unnecessary pots and kettles, for on bacon and flour one can ring but few changes, and it requires but few vessels to cook them. One luxury we had which other emigrants nearly always lacked—fresh milk. From our gentle "mulley" cow I never parted. . . .

Well, on that Monday morning, bright and early, we were off. With the first streak of daylight my last cup of coffee boiled in the wide fire-place,

(continued)

and the sun was scarcely above the horizon when we were on the road to California. The first day's slow jogging brought us to the Missouri River, over which we were ferried in the twilight, and our first camp fire was lighted in Indian Territory, which spread in one unbroken, unnamed waste from the Missouri River to the border line of California. Here commenced my terrors. Around us in every direction were groups of Indians sitting, standing, and on horseback, as many as two hundred in the camp. I had read and heard whole volumes of their bloody deeds, the massacre of harmless white men, torturing helpless women, carrying away captive innocent babes. I felt my children the most precious in the wide world, and I lived in an agony of dread that first night. The Indians were friendly, of course, and swapped ponies for whisky and tobacco with the gathering bands of emigrants, but I, in the most tragi-comic manner, sheltered my babies with my own body, and felt imaginary arrows pierce my flesh a hundred times during the night. At last the morning broke, and we were off. . . . Our train consisted only of six wagons, but we were never alone. Ahead, as far as the eye could reach, a thin cloud of dust marked the route of the trains, and behind us, like the trail of a great serpent, it extended to the edge of civilization. . . .

The traveler who flies across the continent in palace cars, skirting occasionally the old emigrant road, may think that he realizes the trials of such a journey. Nothing but actual experience will give one an idea of the plodding, unvarying monotony, the vexations, the exhaustive energy, the throbs of hope, the depths of despair, through which we lived. Day after day, week after week, we went through the same weary routine of breaking camp at daybreak, yoking the oxen, cooking our meagre rations over a fire of sage-brush and scrub-oak; packing up again, coffeepot and camp-kettle; washing our scanty wardrobe in the little streams we crossed; striking camp again at sunset, or later if wood and water were scarce. Tired, dusty, tried in temper, worn out in patience, we had to go over the weary experience tomorrow. No excitement, but a broken-down wagon, or the extra preparation made to cross a river, marked our way for many miles. The Platte was the first great water-course we crossed. It is a peculiar, wide, shallow stream, with a quicksand bed. With the wagon-bed on blocks twelve or fourteen inches thick to raise it out of the water, some of the men astride of the oxen, some of them wading waist-deep, and all goading the poor beasts to keep them moving, we started across. The water poured into the wagon in spite of our precautions and floated off some of our few movables; but we landed

(continued)

safely on the other side, and turned to see the team behind us stop in mid-stream. The frantic driver shouted, whipped, belabored the stubborn animals in vain, and the treacherous sand gave way under their feet. They sank slowly, gradually, but surely. They went out of sight inch by inch, and the water rose over the moaning beasts. Without a struggle they disappeared beneath the surface. In a little while the broad South Platte swept on its way, sunny, sparkling, placid, without a ripple to mark where a lonely man parted with all his fortune.

Vocabulary

toddling—barely able to walk

comprehensive—complete

prairie schooner—covered wagon

burdensome—creating a heavy load

vessels—containers

emigrants—travelers leaving a place

mulley—a cow with no horns

jogging—going at a slow pace

ferried—carried by boat across a body of water

waste—broad expanse of uncultivated land

commenced—began

skirting—moving along the edge

plodding—slow moving

monotony—boring sameness

vexations—irritations

throbs—pulses

yoking—fastening together at the neck

meagre—small in amount (more commonly spelled *meager* today)

scanty—limited

weary—tiring

astride—with one leg on each side

goading—poking with a pointed rod

precautions—care taken in advance

frantic—emotionally out of control

belabored—beat

treacherous—dangerous

placid—calm

Comprehension Questions

1. Why did Luzena's husband want to leave his family temporarily?

2. Why did he end up bringing his entire family?

3. What did the family expect would happen once they reached California?

4. List the items they believed were necessities at the outset of the journey.

5. How early did they leave?

6. How did the family's covered wagon get across the Missouri River?

7. What frightened Wilson above all else? Why?

8. How did the Indians with whom they came into contact behave?

9. How many wagons were in their train? Were the trails crowded?

10. List the complaints that Wilson had about the overland journey.

11. What precautions were used to keep the contents of the wagon dry when crossing the South Platte River?

12. What happened to the wagon that followed the Wilsons' during the river crossing?

Critical Thinking

1. Was Luzena Wilson's family taking a big risk in going to California? Explain.

2. Why did Wilson think that certain items were necessities but then left them behind on the trail?

3. What did Wilson think of the journey?

4. Why did settlers travel in wagon trains?

5. Luzena Wilson's daughter recorded this memoir in 1881. How might the passage of time since the event have colored Wilson's recollections?

6. How would you describe Wilson's attitude toward the journey?

7. How might a diary Wilson could have written along the way be different from her later recollections?

Making Connections

1. Look at a physical map of the United States. What physical features might present problems to an 1840s wagon train traveling from Missouri to the San Francisco area of California?

2. Find a map that shows the Oregon-California Trail—used by those traveling to the gold rush. Use the map scale to compute the distance from Independence, Missouri, to Sacramento, California.

3. Was Luzena Wilson's fear of the Indians reasonable? Do you think it was fair? Explain.

4. How might a woman's traditional role change on the overland trail?

Relating the Past to Our Lives

1. Imagine you had to leave your home with just the bare necessities for a journey. What three things would you select first?

2. Today California still seems to be a destination for people who want to start a new life. What is there about California today that seems to prompt this optimism?

3. The towns where a wagon train gathered and left from were called "jumping-off points." That's because wagon-train travelers were jumping off into the unknown. What feelings would the prospect of such a journey have created in you?

Essay Questions

1. Write a diary entry of a typical day on the trail to California.

2. Even without the gold rush as a motive, thousands of settlers left their homes to move west. What factors caused people to seek a new start in the West?

3. Historian Frederick Jackson Turner wrote that conquering the frontier formed the American character. What personal qualities did the experience of overcoming the obstacles of traveling west draw on?

Document: Lucretia Mott, "Discourse on Women" (1849)

Historical Context

Most Americans today like to think that when a man and a woman marry, they become one. Ideally, they enter a partnership of shared responsibilities and benefits. In the years before the Civil War, the married couple certainly became one. But the one was the husband. The woman was reduced to zero in the eyes of the law.

Upon marriage, a woman became a "femme covert." This was a legal term meaning that a man takes over or covers his wife's legal identity once married.

• She could not own property, make contracts, or sue.

• She could not divorce her husband.

• She did not even control custody of her children if her husband died.

Of course, she could not vote. Socially, male and female activities were divided into spheres, or areas, of acceptable activity. The husband left the home during the day to be involved in finance, war, law, and politics. He returned home to his wife's area of responsibility. She took care of the home, the children, and morality. The woman's sphere kept her from many activities and placed her at the mercy of her husband in legal matters. In practice, the relationship may have proved more equal in areas such as decision making. But legally the wife remained at her husband's mercy. Even in cases when the husband-wife relationship was good, many women disliked their position. This was especially true in a nation that held rights and liberty in such high regard.

Lucretia Mott was born into a Nantucket, Massachusetts, Quaker family in 1793. As a Quaker, she was exposed to ideas about equality that seem very modern by today's standards. She eventually became an abolitionist and women's rights crusader. An experience at a World Anti-Slavery Convention in England in 1840 pushed her into women's rights. The male organizers of the convention refused to allow the female American delegates to sit in the same room as the men. This was a customary practice in public meetings in both countries.

After the convention, Mott determined that something must be done about the position of women. In 1848, she joined with Elizabeth Cady Stanton to organize a women's rights convention. It was held in Seneca Falls, New York. The women who attended issued a Declaration of Sentiments patterned after the Declaration of Independence. It listed the abuses women suffered at the hands of men. The female participants even pledged to work for a woman's right to vote—a very controversial position at the time. Frederick Douglass, who attended the convention, convinced the women that the vote was necessary to achieve their other goals.

       www.socialstudies.com/walch

Importance

"Discourse on Women" was a speech Mott made in 1849 later published as a pamphlet. It was a response to a male lecturer who criticized women's demand for equal rights. This critical lecture surely was inspired by the recent the Seneca Falls Convention. The speech reflects the ideas discussed in New York a year earlier. The immediate response by most men to both the convention and the pamphlet was ridicule. Mott was too radical for most women also. Nonetheless, at least some of her ideas hit home with many women. They may not have wanted to vote, but divorce and property rights were important to many. "Discourse on Women" is a particularly effective argument in its logic and clarity.

Lucretia Mott, "Discourse on Women," 1849

The question is often asked, "What does woman want, more than she enjoys? What is she seeking to obtain? Of what rights is she deprived? What privileges are withheld from her? I answer, she asks nothing as favor, but as right, she wants to be acknowledged a moral, responsible being. She is seeking not to be governed by laws, in the making of which she has no voice. She is deprived of almost every right in civil society, and is a cypher in the nation, except in the right of presenting a petition. In religious society her disabilities, as already pointed out, have greatly retarded her progress. Her exclusion from the pulpit or ministry — her duties marked out for her by her equal brother man, subject to creeds, rules, and disciplines made for her by him — this is unworthy her true dignity. In marriage, there is assumed superiority, on the part of the husband, and admitted inferiority, with a promise of obedience, on the part of the wife. This subject calls loudly for examination, in order that the wrong may be redressed. Customs suited to darker ages in Eastern countries, are not binding upon enlightened society. The solemn covenant of marriage may be entered into without these lordly assumptions, and humiliating concessions and promises. . . .

So with woman. She has so long been subject to the disabilities and restrictions, with which her progress has been embarrassed, that she has become enervated, her mind to some extent paralysed; and, like those still more degraded by personal bondage, she hugs her chains. Liberty is often presented in its true light, but it is liberty for man. . . .

Walker, of Cincinnati, in his *Introduction to American Law*, says: . . . "The law of husband and wife, as you gather it from the books,

(continued)

is a disgrace to any civilized nation. The theory of the law degrades the wife almost to the level of slaves. When a woman marries, we call her condition coverture, and speak of her as a *femme covert*. The old writers call the husband baron, and sometimes, in plain English, lord. The merging of her name in that of her husband is emblematic of the fate of all her legal rights. The torch of Hymen serves but to light the pile, on which these rights are offered up. The legal theory is, that marriage makes the husband and wife one person, and that person is the *husband*. On this subject, reform is loudly called for. There is no foundation in reason or expediency, for the absolute and slavish subjection of the wife to the husband, which forms the foundation of the present legal relations. Were woman, in point of fact, the abject thing which the law, in theory, considers her to be when married, she would not be worthy the companionship of man." . . .

There are many instances now in our city, where the wife suffers much from the power of the husband to claim all that she can earn with her own hands. In my intercourse with the poorer class of people, I have known cases of extreme cruelty, from the hard earnings of the wife being thus robbed by the husband, and no redress at law. . . .

Let woman then go on — not asking as favor, but claiming as right, the removal of all the hindrances to her elevation in the scale of being — let her receive encouragement for the proper cultivation of all her powers, so that she may enter profitably into the active business of life; . . .

Vocabulary

acknowledged—recognized

deprived—withheld

cypher—person without worth

disabilities—disqualifications

exclusion—prevention from participation

pulpit—high reading desk used in a worship service

creeds—beliefs

examination—close study

redressed—made right

binding—required to be followed

enlightened—freed from misinformation

solemn covenant—serious agreement

assumptions—concepts taken for granted

concessions—things given up

enervated—reduced in strength

paralysed—made powerless (this is the British spelling; the American spelling is *paralyzed*)

degraded—greatly lowered in status

bondage—slavery

coverture—legal status of woman upon marriage

femme covert—legal term for a married woman; describes her status

emblematic—representative

Hymen—the Greek God of marriage

expediency—choosing the way most helpful to oneself

slavish—like a slave

subjection—state of being under the control of another

abject—existing in a low condition

intercourse—social interaction

hindrances—things that make action difficult

elevation—upgrading

cultivation—development

Comprehension Questions

1. List the complaints Mott makes regarding the position of women.

2. Mott compares the status of American women to the status of women of what foreign region?

3. What does Mott think bad treatment has done to women's thinking abilities?

4. What happens to the legal rights of women upon marriage?

5. What does Mott think needs to happen about women's rights after marriage?

6. Since a man owns the wife's property, what can happen to the wife's wages?

7. What two things does Mott want for women?

Critical Thinking

1. What do you think of Mott's argument? Explain.

2. Who do you think is Mott's intended audience?

3. What is Mott's purpose?

4. When Mott says a woman "hugs her chains," what does she mean?

5. Several times, Mott compares the wife's position with that of a slave. Why do you think she does that?

Making Connections

1. To achieve Mott's purpose, who needs to take action? Why?

2. Why does Mott suggest that the case of a husband taking a wife's wages happens only among poor people?

3. How does Mott being a Quaker influence her position about women's rights?

4. How do you think men would react to Mott's ideas? Why?

5. Why do you think women accepted their position in society for so long?

Relating the Past to Our Lives

1. Imagine your life if you could not own property or have a driver's license or collect a paycheck in your name. How would that change your life?

2. Do women have legal rights equal to those of men today? Are they equal in every other way? Explain.

3. Women who actively worked for women's rights formed a tiny minority in Mott's time. Have you ever been part of such a small group that was trying to change majority opinion for some controversial issue? Explain.

Essay Questions

1. Many who tried to improve a woman's position in society at the time began as abolitionists. Why do you think that is?

2. Which of the rights Mott discusses do you think was most important to women at the time? Explain.

3. Do you think Mott speaks in an angry tone in "Discourse"? Explain.

The Compromise of 1850

Document: Henry Clay, Resolutions (January 29, 1850)

Historical Context

Compromises are supposed to leave the parties involved reasonably happy with the outcome. Usually each side gives a little and gains something in return. This give-and-take was true with the Compromise of 1850. Yet this compromise left more angry feelings than satisfaction.

Due to the 1849 California gold rush, the new California territory's population had increased very rapidly. Enough people lived there to qualify for its admission as a state in 1850. This presented a problem. California outlawed slavery within its boundaries. The new state of California upset the balance of free states and slave states that had been in place for thirty years.

In 1820 when Missouri citizens petitioned Congress for statehood, slavery was legal in Missouri. Many in Congress objected. As a state, Missouri would add two members to the U.S. Senate. A majority of senators would then represent the slave states. With the leadership of Speaker of the House Henry Clay, the Missouri Compromise was reached. Under the terms of the Compromise, Missouri became the eleventh slave state. At the same time, Maine entered the Union as the eleventh free state. A line indicated the future of slavery in the remaining territory. States created from the territory north of 36° 30' north latitude must outlaw slavery. States created from land to the south of this line could allow slavery. After 1820, states entering the Union kept the slave state/free state balance close to even.

A lot of new territory was gained in 1848 as a result of the Mexican War. The possibility of new states created from this land raised new tensions. When California requested statehood as a free state, a crisis greater than in 1820 followed. Several reasons prompted this crisis:

- No other territory had the population at this time to become a slave state to maintain the balance as it was.

- Tensions over slavery had increased a great deal since 1820. There was even talk of Southern states leaving the Union over California.

Henry Clay was now a seventy-year-old U.S. senator. Once again he tried to create an acceptable compromise. He introduced a bill in January 1850. It contained a series of resolutions. Some parts were favorable to the North, some to the South. The highlights were as follows:

- For the North, California would become a free state. Also, the selling and buying of slaves in Washington, D.C., was outlawed.

- For the South, slavery remained legal in Washington, D.C. Most important, Congress would pass a tougher fugitive slave law. It would strictly require runaway slaves to be returned to the South.

- In the new territory aside from California, the voters of any new states would decide the slavery question.

Clay's bill failed to pass because Northern and Southern congressmen united to oppose it—for different reasons. Seeing this, Senator Stephen Douglas divided the parts of the compromise into separate bills. Each had enough support to pass.

Importance

This compromise between opposing sections of the country was different from those that came before. Because it passed in pieces, few congressmen voted for every part. Clay's original resolutions presented here had failed. The final outcome seemed less a settlement than a postponement of a confrontation. It left Northerners furious over the Fugitive Slave Act. In turn, Southerners were angry over the new imbalance in the Senate.

Henry Clay, Resolutions, January 29, 1850

It being desirable, for the peace, concord, and harmony of the Union of these States, to settle and adjust amicably all existing questions of controversy between them arising out of the institution of slavery upon a fair, equitable and just basis: therefore,

1. Resolved, That California, with suitable boundaries, ought, upon her application to be admitted as one of the States of this Union, without the imposition by Congress of any restriction in respect to the exclusion or introduction of slavery within those boundaries.

2. Resolved, That as slavery does not exist by law, and is not likely to be introduced into any of the territory acquired by the United States from the republic of Mexico, it is inexpedient for Congress to provide by law either for its introduction into, or exclusion from, any part of the said territory; and that appropriate territorial governments ought to be established by Congress in all of the said territory, not assigned as the boundaries of the proposed State of California, without the adoption of any restriction or condition on the subject of slavery.

(continued)

3. Resolved, That the western boundary of the State of Texas ought to be fixed on the Rio del Norte, commencing one marine league from its mouth, and running up that river to the southern line of New Mexico; thence with that line eastwardly, and so continuing in the same direction to the line as established between the United States and Spain, excluding any portion of New Mexico, whether lying on the east or west of that river.

4. Resolved, That it be proposed to the State of Texas, that the United States will provide for the payment of all that portion of the legitimate and bona fide public debt of that State contracted prior to its annexation to the United States, . . . upon the condition, also, that the said State of Texas shall, by some solemn and authentic act of her legislature or of a convention, relinquish to the United States any claim which it has to any part of New Mexico.

5. Resolved, That it is inexpedient to abolish slavery in the District of Columbia whilst that institution continues to exist in the State of Maryland, without the consent of that State, without the consent of the people of the District, and without just compensation to the owners of slaves within the District.

6. But, resolved, That it is expedient to prohibit, within the District, the slave trade in slaves brought into it from States or places beyond the limits of the District, either to be sold therein as merchandise, or to be transported to other markets without the District of Columbia.

7. Resolved, That more effectual provision ought to be made by law, according to the requirement of the constitution, for the restitution and delivery of persons bound to service or labor in any State, who may escape into any other State or Territory in the Union. And,

8. Resolved, That Congress has no power to promote or obstruct the trade in slaves between the slaveholding States; but that the admission or exclusion of slaves brought from one into another of them depends exclusively upon their own particular laws.

Vocabulary

concord—state of agreement

amicably—in a friendly manner

equitable—dealing fairly with all concerned

admitted—allowed to join

imposition—uncalled-for requirement

exclusion—preventing the entrance of

inexpedient—not advisable

commencing—beginning

marine league—a unit of distance on the sea

portion—part

bona fide—made honestly

contracted—made by a binding agreement

relinquish—to give up

consent—agreement

compensation—something given to balance a loss

expedient—advisable

prohibit—to forbid

therein—in that place

merchandise—item for sale

without—outside

effectual—effective

provision—a measure taken beforehand

restitution—return to a former condition

obstruct—to block

exclusively—solely

Comprehension Questions

1. Who proposed the resolutions?

2. What was their purpose?

3. How is Congress resolving to handle California and slavery, according to the first resolution?

4. In the remaining territory gained from Mexico, what will territorial governments do regarding slavery?

5. What issue does the third resolution deal with?

6. What exchange does Congress offer Texas?

7. What makes the abolition of slavery in Washington, D.C., a bad idea, according to the fifth resolution?

8. What aspect of slavery will be ended if the resolutions pass?

9. Resolution 7 states that a law should be passed to accomplish what?

10. How will slavery be treated in states where it currently exists?

Critical Thinking

1. Since California requested statehood as a free state, what does Congress's position on slavery in the first resolution mean for California?

2. How will the slavery question be answered in the remaining territories gained from Mexico?

3. Why would the Northern states care about eliminating the slave trade in Washington, D.C.?

4. In resolution 7, what group of people does "persons bound to service or labor" refer to?

5. Which resolutions are designed to please the slave states? the free states?

Making Connections

1. List several other compromises that have been significant in U.S. history.

2. List the six states that entered the Union after the Missouri Compromise and before the Compromise of 1850.

3. Aside from slavery, what other differences existed between the Northern and Southern states?

4. Why did the Missouri Compromise line not apply to the new territory?

5. What made people who opposed slavery accept this compromise?

6. Why could Congress make decisions concerning slavery in the territories and in Washington, D.C., but not in the states?

Relating the Past to Our Lives

1. Have you ever compromised with someone over an important issue? Explain.

2. What would you never compromise about?

3. Compromises are often necessary in politics. Can you think of a recent political compromise made to settle an important issue?

Essay Questions

1. Abraham Lincoln said, "I believe this government cannot endure permanently half slave and half free." Were compromises such as the Compromise of 1850 doomed to fail? Explain.

2. Compromises are necessary for governments to operate. Can compromises have a negative effect? Explain.

3. Propose another compromise that could have permanently smoothed tensions between North and South.

4. Compare the Compromise of 1850 with the Missouri Compromise.

"The Nature of Slavery"

Document: Frederick Douglass, "The Nature of Slavery" (1850)

Historical Context

Can a man steal himself? That is what Frederick Douglass said he did when he escaped from slavery in Maryland. In 1838 at the age of twenty, he stole himself from his owner and fled north. He became the nation's most important black intellectual of the 1800s.

Once free, Douglass began speaking at antislavery meetings around New Bedford, Massachusetts, where he lived. He quickly became a sensation. Boston abolitionist William Lloyd Garrison soon enlisted Douglass to lecture and contribute to Garrison's abolitionist newspaper, *The Liberator*. Douglass told Northern audiences about slavery from firsthand experience. He did this with impressive use of language. Douglass had no formal education. But he secretly taught himself to read and write.

- While Douglass was a child, his master's wife taught him the alphabet. Her husband found out and made her stop the lessons. In most slave states it was illegal to teach a slave to read.

- Later Douglass traded food with neighborhood white boys for reading and writing lessons.

- Once Douglass could read, he educated himself. He stole opportunities to read the newspaper when no one was looking.

- At the age of twelve, Douglass got hold of a copy of *The Columbian Orator*, a popular schoolbook. This helped him understand the power of words.

Douglass's eloquence was exceptional, even for an educated white person. Therefore, some people doubted that Douglass had ever been a slave. They accused him of being an educated free black pretending to be an ex-slave.

Douglass decided to offer proof, even though many abolitionist friends urged him not to. The truth of his words was at stake. Between 1844 and 1845, he wrote *Narrative of the Life of Frederick Douglass, an American Slave*. In it Douglass revealed his real name—Frederick Bailey. He had changed his name to Douglass so that he could not be found by slave catchers. Under fugitive slave law, his master could legally return him to slavery in Maryland. Revealing his identity proved his previous enslavement but put his freedom in danger. He had to leave the country to be safe.

Douglass sailed to Great Britain soon after *Narrative* was published in 1845. While he was there, the British praised his work. In 1846, two British admirers purchased his freedom, paying his former master $710.96. Upon his return to the United States, Douglass settled in Rochester, New York. Differences arose between him and Garrison. So Douglass began publishing his own abolitionist newspaper, *The North Star*.

Importance

Douglass made this speech in Rochester to a hometown audience—one probably sympathetic to his views. By 1850, Douglass had been an abolitionist for over twenty years. The last paragraph refers to a peace settlement—the Compromise of 1850, passed three months before the speech. It was the last of several attempts to settle differences between North and South over the expansion of slavery. Under the terms of the Compromise, California entered the Union as a free state. In return, Congress passed a stronger fugitive slave law.

Frederick Douglass, "The Nature of Slavery," December 1, 1850

More than twenty years of my life were consumed in a state of slavery. My childhood was environed by the baneful peculiarities of the slave system. I grew up to manhood in the presence of this hydra-headed monster—not as a master—not as an idle spectator—not as the guest of the slaveholder—but as A SLAVE, eating the bread and drinking the cup of slavery with the most degraded of my brother-bondmen, and sharing with them all the painful conditions of their wretched lot. In consideration of these facts, I feel that I have a right to speak, and to speak *strongly*. Yet, my friends, I feel bound to speak truly. . . .

First of all, I will state, as well as I can, the legal and social relation of master and slave. A master is one—to speak in the vocabulary of the southern states—who claims and exercises a right of property in the person of a fellow-man. This he does with the force of the law and the sanction of southern religion. The law gives the master absolute power over the slave. He may work him, flog him, hire him out, sell him, and, in certain contingencies, *kill* him, with perfect impunity. The slave is a human being, divested of all rights—reduced to the level of a brute—a mere "chattel" in the eye of the law—placed beyond the circle of human brotherhood—cut off from his kind—his name, which the "recording angel" may have enrolled in heaven, among the blest, is impiously inserted in a *master's ledger,* with horses, sheep, and swine. In law, the slave has no wife, no children, no country, and no home. He can own nothing, possess nothing, acquire nothing, but what must belong to another. . . .

(continued)

The slave is a man, "the image of God," but "a little lower than the angels;" possessing a soul, eternal and indestructible; capable of endless happiness, or immeasurable woe; a creature of hopes and fears, of affections and passions, of joys and sorrows, and he is endowed with those mysterious powers by which man soars above the things of time and sense, and grasps, with undying tenacity, the elevating and sublimely glorious idea of a God. It is *such* a being that is smitten and blasted. The first work of slavery is to mar and deface those characteristics of its victims which distinguish *men* from *things,* and *persons* from *property.* Its first aim is to destroy all sense of high moral and religious responsibility. It reduces man to a mere machine. It cuts him off from his Maker, it hides from him the laws of God, and leaves him to grope his way from time to eternity in the dark, under the arbitrary and despotic control of a frail, depraved, and sinful fellow-man. . . .

The great mass of slaveholders look upon education among the slaves as utterly subversive of the slave system. I well remember when my mistress first announced to my master that she had discovered that I could read. His face colored at once with surprise and chagrin. He said that "I was ruined, and my value as a slave destroyed; that a slave should know nothing but to obey his master; that to give a negro an inch would lead him to take an ell; that having learned how to read, I would soon want to know how to write; and that by-and-by I would be running away." I think my audience will bear witness to the correctness of this philosophy, and to the literal fulfillment of this prophecy. . . .

While this nation is guilty of the enslavement of three millions of innocent men and women, it is as idle to think of having a sound and lasting peace, as it is to think there is no God to take cognizance of the affairs of men. There can be no peace to the wicked while slavery continues in the land. It will be condemned; and while it is condemned there will be agitation. Nature must cease to be nature; men must become monsters; humanity must be transformed; christianity must be exterminated; all ideas of justice and the laws of eternal goodness must be utterly blotted out from the human soul, —ere a system so foul and infernal can escape condemnation, or this guilty republic can have a sound, enduring peace.

Vocabulary

environed—surrounded

baneful—harmful

hydra-headed monster—many-sided source of destruction

idle—unoccupied

degraded—reduced in self-worth

bondmen—slaves

wretched—extremely bad

bound—obliged

sanction—approval by authority

absolute—complete

flog—to whip

contingencies—situations

impunity—freedom from punishment

divested—deprived

brute—animal

chattel—property

impiously—in a manner lacking in respect for God

inserted—put in

ledger—a book containing purchases and sales

eternal—never-ending

immeasurable woe—unhappiness beyond measure

endowed with—given

tenacity—the quality of never giving up

elevating—uplifting

sublimely—grandly

mar—damage

grope—feel your way blindly

arbitrary—based on individual preference and not fixed by law

despotic—having complete power

frail—weak

depraved—morally bad

subversive—having the ability to overthrow

chagrin—distress

ell—unit of measure equal to 45 inches

bear witness—to provide evidence for

philosophy—system of thought

literal—actual

prophecy—prediction

cognizance—knowledge; awareness

agitation—excitement

exterminated—destroyed

utterly—completely

ere—before

infernal—relating to hell

condemnation—blame

Comprehension Questions

1. How long was Douglass a slave?

2. What two authorities give permission for slavery to exist, according to Douglass?

3. What degree of power does a master have over the slave?

4. What does a slave have under U.S. law?

5. What human qualities does Douglass remind the audience the slave has?

6. What is the first job of the slave owner?

7. By cutting the slave off from God, what is the slave owner doing, according to Douglass?

8. What do slaveholders think of educating slaves?

9. According to Douglass, why can the nation not be at peace?

Critical Thinking

1. What is the legal status of the slave in the South, according to Douglass?

2. When Douglass says that slavery reduces "man to a mere machine," what does he mean?

3. How important was it to his message for Douglass to have been a slave himself? Explain.

4. Why do you think Douglass was so determined to learn to read?

5. Why was a lasting peace impossible with slavery still legal, according to Douglass?

6. Assess the speech. What qualities make the speech persuasive?

Making Connections

1. Douglass once wrote that slavery corrupts the slaveholder. What did he mean by that?

2. Douglass includes many references to religion in this speech. Why do you think he does this?

3. Frederick Douglass was clearly the most important black leader of his time. Judging from his speech, what personal qualities made him so respected?

Relating the Past to Our Lives

1. What would Douglass have to say about the place of African Americans in today's society?

2. Can you name the spokesperson for a social cause today? What does the person do to communicate his or her message?

3. What leader inspires you? What qualities does he or she have?

Essay Questions

1. In his first autobiography, Douglass writes that no one can be enslaved if he has the ability to read and write. Do you agree? Explain.

2. How is Douglass's experience in slavery similar to the experience of Olaudah Equiano? How is it different?

3. At the end of the speech, Douglass makes a reference to a lasting peace in the nation being impossible while slavery still exists. This refers to the Compromise of 1850. It supposedly settled tensions between the North and the South over the expansion of slavery. Do you agree that there was no way to make a lasting settlement between the contending sides?

The Gettysburg Address

Document: Abraham Lincoln, the Gettysburg Address (1863)

Historical Context

Two hundred thirty-six words is not a long speech even by today's standards. It was far shorter by the standards of the nineteenth century. But the speech was supposed to be short. It was the official dedication of the Gettysburg cemetery—not the main event. The main event was to be an oration by Edward Everett of Massachusetts. This lasted over two hours before an audience of 15,000 at Gettysburg, Pennsylvania, on November 19, 1863. President Lincoln's three-minute speech, however, was the one considered among the greatest in American history. This short speech later became known as the Gettysburg Address.

Four months earlier on July 1–3, the Union Army of the Potomac had defeated the Confederate Army of Northern Virginia at Gettysburg. This ended the Confederates' attempt to win on Northern soil. The battle left 51,000 wounded, killed, captured, or missing between the two armies. Confederate General Robert E. Lee's army would never be the same. On July 4, the Confederate-controlled city of Vicksburg, Mississippi, fell to a Union army. This victory gave the North control of the Mississippi River. The tide of war now firmly favored the North.

At the November event, a part of the Gettysburg battlefield was being made into a national cemetery. Lincoln was invited to make "a few appropriate remarks" as a representative of the national government. This would make the opening of the national cemetery official. The President's role was similar to a ribbon-cutting ceremony today. But Lincoln understood the importance of the occasion, and he wanted his words to be equally important. Although the war lasted for two more years, the outcome was no longer in doubt. Lincoln wanted what he said to be memorable.

Lincoln did not write his speech on the back of an envelope on the train to Gettysburg as is popularly believed. He worked on it at the White House, trying to get the words just right. Lincoln's speech received favorable reviews from Northern newspapers. Yet, in the end, Lincoln believed his speech had failed.

Importance

The Gettysburg Address paid tribute to the men who died in the battle. But Lincoln did not mention North or South, Union or Confederate. Nor did he address slavery. He also did not celebrate what appeared to be an eventual Union victory in the war. Lincoln had goals that went beyond the present problems. He wanted his words to be about American ideals. Some say he redefined these ideals in the speech by using the words of the Declaration of

Independence as the founding law of the nation—not the Constitution, which allowed slavery. In this way, the speech looked back at the nation's founding ideals, and it looked forward to an important war aim. This Lincoln called "a new birth of freedom." The Fourteenth and Fifteenth Amendments were passed after Lincoln's death. They were intended to give newly freed African Americans the rights of citizenship—a new birth of freedom.

Abraham Lincoln, Gettysburg Address, November 19, 1863

Executive Mansion,

Washington, 1863

Fourscore and seven years ago our fathers brought forth on this continent a new nation, conceived in liberty and dedicated to the proposition that all men are created equal.

Now we are engaged in a great civil war, testing whether that nation or any nation so conceived and so dedicated can long endure. We are met on a great battlefield of that war. We have come to dedicate a portion of it as a final resting place for those who died here that the nation might live. This we may, in all propriety do. But in a larger sense, we cannot dedicate, we cannot consecrate, we cannot hallow this ground. The brave men, living and dead who struggled here have hallowed it far above our poor power to add or detract. The world will little note nor long remember what we say here, but it can never forget what they did here.

It is rather for us the living, to here be dedicated to the great task remaining before us—that from these honored dead we take increased devotion to that cause for which they here gave the last full measure of devotion—that we here highly resolve that these dead shall not have died in vain, that this nation shall have a new birth of freedom, and that government of the people, by the people, for the people shall not perish from the earth.

Vocabulary

fourscore—eighty years

conceived—began

proposition—idea for consideration

engaged—involved

endure—to continue

portion—part

propriety—properness

consecrate—to make sacred

hallow—to make holy

detract—to lessen in importance

note—to notice

devotion—being dedicated

measure—amount

resolve—to firmly decide

in vain—needlessly

perish—to become destroyed

Comprehension Questions

1. If a score is twenty years, how many years is four score and seven? What event is Lincoln referring to?

2. What two ideas was the United States dedicated to making true, according to Lincoln?

3. What is the Civil War testing?

4. What is the purpose of the gathering Lincoln is speaking to?

5. What have the deaths of the soldiers done for the cemetery?

6. Does Lincoln believe his words will be remembered?

7. What will the world remember?

8. What should the living do?

Critical Thinking

1. What does Lincoln mean when he says "our fathers"?

2. Why does Lincoln include words from the Declaration of Independence?

3. Why does Lincoln date the beginning of the country from the Declaration of Independence and not from the Constitution?

4. What does Lincoln mean by a "new birth of freedom"?

5. What do you think about Lincoln's use of language in the speech?

Making Connections

1. Where do the words "all men are created equal" come from?

2. Why did Lincoln make a speech such as this after the battle of Gettysburg and the siege of Vicksburg?

3. Why did Lincoln avoid mentioning either side in the war?

Relating the Past to Our Lives

1. Have you ever been to a dedication ceremony? What was it for? What were the parts to the ceremony?

2. Does your town have a memorial to soldiers' service in past wars? Spend time examining it. Which war is it for? Is it in a place where it can be seen easily? What does the inscription say?

3. Have any of your relatives served in a war? Do you think his or her service is appreciated?

Essay Questions

1. Confederate soldiers were also buried at the Gettysburg cemetery. Write a response to Lincoln's speech from a Confederate soldier's point of view.

2. Why do you think the Gettysburg Address is one of the most famous in American history?

3. What can the Gettysburg Address say to us today?

4. Some say that Lincoln made the ideals of the Declaration of Independence part of the Constitution in this speech. Do you agree? Explain.

The Reconstruction Amendments

Document: The Thirteenth, Fourteenth, and Fifteenth Amendments to the U.S. Constitution (1865–1870)

Historical Context

Abraham Lincoln was assassinated before he could help create the "new birth of freedom" he referred to in his Gettysburg Address. Aside from the end of slavery, it is not clear what Lincoln had in mind for the former slaves after the war. John Wilkes Booth shot Lincoln on April 14, 1865; the president died the next morning. The job of rebuilding the nation was then left for Congress and Lincoln's successor, Vice President Andrew Johnson.

After the Civil War ended, the nation had to "reconstruct" the country—make it whole again. In order to do this, two main objectives had to be achieved:

1. *Unify the country.* Set the conditions under which Southern states could return to the Union. These states had seceded, or formally separated from the United States, to form the Confederate States of America. To be represented in the U.S. Congress again, the former Confederate states needed to rejoin the Union. Many Northerners wanted this to happen in order to reestablish business connections. Others wanted to punish the South by keeping it out of the Union.

2. *Help the freed slaves begin new lives.* Lincoln's Emancipation Proclamation of 1862 had freed most of the Confederacy's slaves by war's end. But slaves in the slave states that had stayed in the Union remained enslaved—until the Thirteenth Amendment. After freedom, what other rights should African Americans gain in order to have a fair chance for a productive life?

An amendment is a permanent change in the U.S. Constitution. Consequently, the requirements for adding an amendment are high. Most amendments have been passed by two-thirds votes of both houses of Congress followed by approval of three fourths of the states. The Reconstruction Amendments followed that process.

- The Thirteenth Amendment (1865) outlawed slavery throughout the United States. Slavery had been legal under the Constitution. So an amendment was needed to ban slavery.

- The Fourteenth Amendment (1868) was designed to give equal citizenship to African Americans by preventing states from denying their rights. This amendment became necessary after Southern states passed Black Codes creating a second-class citizenship for blacks. Segregation laws later weakened the Fourteenth Amendment. The Supreme Court did not consider "separate but equal" laws a violation of the amendment for nearly a hundred years.

- The Fifteenth Amendment (1870) was designed to give black men the right to vote.

 www.socialstudies.com/walch

Many women who had worked as abolitionists felt betrayed when they were left out of this expansion of voting rights. Later, Southern states created laws that prevented most of their African-American men from voting. These laws were worded so they could be interpreted as not directly violating the Fifteenth Amendment's wording.

Importance

The goals of unifying the country and bringing justice to freed slaves often clashed. Most white Southerners did not want rights for African Americans. Most Northerners didn't care about the issue. Southern states denied African Americans the full meaning of the Fourteenth and Fifteenth Amendments for years. It took the Civil Rights Act of 1964 and the Voting Rights Act of 1965 for the amendments to be enforced. That was over a hundred years since they had become part of the Constitution. The civil rights leaders of the 1950s and 1960s pointed out that the rights they sought were already guaranteed by the Constitution. This made it easier to get laws passed to enforce those guarantees.

Reconstruction Amendments, 1865, 1868, 1870

Amendment XIII

Section 1. Neither slavery nor involuntary servitude, except as a punishment for crime whereof the party shall have been duly convicted, shall exist within the United States, or any place subject to their jurisdiction. . . .

Amendment XIV

Section 1. All persons born or naturalized in the United States, and subject to the jurisdiction thereof, are citizens of the United States and of the State wherein they reside. No State shall make or enforce any law which shall abridge the privileges or immunities of citizens of the United States; nor shall any State deprive any person of life, liberty, or property, without due process of law; nor deny to any person within its jurisdiction the equal protection of the laws. . . .

Amendment XV

Section 1. The right of citizens of the United States to vote shall not be denied or abridged by the United States or by any State on account of race, color, or previous condition of servitude.

Vocabulary

involuntary servitude—working against one's will

whereof—of which

duly—properly

jurisdiction—limits within in which authority may be used

naturalized—allowed to become a citizen though the process stated by law

thereof—of that

wherein—where

abridge—to reduce, to restrict

immunities—protections

deprive—to take away

due process—set of rules

Comprehension Questions

1. What cannot exist in the United States as a result of the Thirteenth Amendment?

2. List the two ways someone can become a U.S. citizen.

3. Which government is the Fourteenth Amendment intended to limit?

4. What is that government prevented from doing?

5. As a result of the Fifteenth Amendment, what cannot be considered in determining who votes?

Critical Thinking

1. What kind of a document is this?

2. These amendments are written in negative language. In other words, they seem to be limitations on government more than a positive granting of freedom. Why was that necessary?

3. Why do you think these three amendments were passed in this order in history?

4. What rights make up due process of law? Why is due process important?

Making Connections

1. Why was an amendment to end slavery necessary despite the Emancipation Proclamation?

2. Reading these amendments, what impression do you get regarding the rights of African Americans in the 1860s?

3. The Fifteenth Amendment lists reasons for which a person cannot be prevented from voting. What reasons are omitted?

4. Which of the three amendments did the Southern states accept without making efforts to weaken it?

5. Does being a citizen give a person the right to vote? Give some evidence to prove your answer.

Relating the Past to Our Lives

1. Have you ever been in a situation where you felt others, no more deserving than you, were given more rights and privileges? How did that feel?

2. Can you think of any groups today that could use laws to protect their rights? Who?

3. The Fourteenth Amendment today is the basis of more court cases than any other of the Constitution's amendments. Why do you think that is?

Essay Questions

1. Lincoln spoke of a "new birth of freedom" once the Civil War ended. How do these amendments intend to fulfill this goal?

2. After these amendments were passed, Southern states were able to create laws that took away rights that were intended to be granted by the Fourteenth and Fifteenth Amendments. How could this happen?

3. What do you think women's rights leaders thought when women's right to vote was left out of the Fifteenth Amendment, especially after many worked so hard to end slavery? What might these women have said at the time?

4. Why did racism not end after these amendments became the law of the land?

Answer Key

The Mayflower Compact

Comprehension Questions

1. The purpose was to plant a colony.
2. They intended to land in northern Virginia. They ended up on Cape Cod in Massachusetts.
3. They combine to better plant an organized, safe colony.
4. They promise to obey the wishes of the group.
5. They signed the compact on November 11, 1620.
6. The signers were all male.

Critical Thinking

1. This was an agreement they wanted heavenly and worldly sanction for. All signers were religious, and the English king granted the land (although, because they went off course, not the land they were on).
2. The main idea is that the will of the majority will control decision making.
3. The audience is the signers themselves.
4. The most important idea is majority rule.
5. There may have been competition for a dominant leader.
6. It is considered an early example of our democratic impulse.

Making Connections

Answers will vary. Sample answers:

1. It is a democratic document to the extent that it agrees to majority rule, but only the men agreed.
2. At the time, a vote by a man was considered one for his family. A family has one vote; the man makes it.
3. The *Mayflower* travelers were particularly concerned because there were two conflicting religious groups present. That was not true in Jamestown. But by 1619, earlier than the *Mayflower*'s landing, the Jamestown groups had created the first representative legislature in America.
4. The Quakers, Amish, and Catholics are a few.
5. Today, historians think people in the past made a bit too much of it. The signers were only continuing something accepted in England for a long time. But it is still considered one of our founding documents.

Relating the Past to Our Lives

1. Answers will vary. Sample answer: It sets an overriding rule for the ways problems will be handled in the future. There is no way to predict the problems, but at least the way they are handled can be established.
2. Answers will vary.
3. Answers will vary.

Essay Questions

Essays will vary.

1. Essays may include laws regarding food, protection, and electing a leader.
2. Essays may state that when a country looks back at its history, it tries to trace the roots of its present institutions. The United States is proud of its democratic foundation.
3. Essays may include fear as a factor. Fear of Indians and other unknown elements can cause people to see what they have in common more easily. Religion was a dividing factor, as was the reason the two groups came to Plymouth. The compact set a standard process that all had agreed to, bringing the group into agreement over something critical to the colony's success.

Common Sense

Comprehension Questions

1. America has done well economically as a colony. It would have done well regardless, since its commerce involved things other countries needed.
2. Britain did it to protect its own interests, not those of the colonies.
3. Britain should be ashamed of the present war in the colonies.
4. Europe is the parent of America. Americans come from a wide variety of European countries.
5. He challenges them to name an advantage that the American colonies would enjoy by remaining part of the British Empire.
6. The colonies should separate because of the disadvantages of remaining a colony and the

colonies' responsibility to the world.

7. It will draw the colonies into conflicts with other countries against whom America has no quarrel or complaint.

8. It will hurt trade relations.

9. Answers will vary.

Critical Thinking

1. The purpose was to make an argument for independence.

2. Answers will vary. Sample answer: Paine wanted to show that separating from Britain made common sense.

3. Answers will vary. Sample answer: One advantage was the protection of the British Empire against attack.

4. It could draw the colonies into wars with other countries and/or hurt their trade.

5. Answers will vary. Examples of Paine's language include the following: that Britain would have defended Turkey for the same reasons it defended the colonies; saying that Britain treated the colonies with the cruelty of a monster.

6. Answers will vary. Sample answer: He argues by analogy and by anticipating the argument of the opposition, then countering it, which are effective techniques.

Making Connections

1. Answers will vary. Books may include *Uncle Tom's Cabin, A Century of Dishonor,* and *Silent Spring.*

2. Answers will vary. Sample answers: Yes, the ethnicity of the colonies is more diverse than in most other countries in Europe. No, because the institutions developed are directly linked to England.

3. Answers will vary. Sample answer: Without British control, the American colonies could have traded directly, and therefore more profitably, with countries other than Britain. British control provided predictable markets and the protection of Britain's powerful navy.

4. He is referring to the French and Indian War.

5. Answers will vary. Sample answer: Another document that makes a reference to natural rights is the Declaration of Independence.

Relating the Past to Our Lives

1. Answers will vary.

2. Answers will vary. Sample answer: It is probably less likely because of the competition from other forms of communication and entertainment.

3. Answers will vary. Sample answer: The words "common sense" imply that the ideas promoted are established as accepted wisdom.

Essay Questions

Essays will vary.

1. Essays may include Paine's understanding of Enlightenment political theory. Many forward-thinking people in Europe saw a republic as a preferred form of government. But it would be an experiment, one that, if successful, might have a ripple effect throughout the world.

2. Essays may include that accepting an agreement with Britain to remove the hated legislation might have been enough to move the moderates in the colonies to vote against independence. The Olive Branch Petition sent by the Second Continental Congress in 1775 was an attempt to do just that. Paine may have had it in mind.

3. Essays may touch on the protection offered by the British, the British roots of many colonists, and the commercial ties between the two that would surely be disrupted with independence.

"Remember the Ladies"

Comprehension Questions

1. She wants the Congress to declare independence.

2. She wants American women to be considered.

3. She fears that men, American husbands, have "unlimited power."

4. They may rebel.

5. She says they are oppressive rulers, tyrants.

6. They need protection from mean and abusive men.

7. He says it makes him laugh.

8. Men will never give up their power, but he also believes the power is more theory than real.

Critical Thinking

1. She is speaking for women in general. In particular, she is concerned about women

married to husbands who exercise absolute
power.

2. "Our Struggle" is the rebellion against Great
Britain.

3. Children, students, apprentices, Indians, and
African Americans (probably he means slaves)
have all requested more rights. They are all in a
position of being "ruled" by others.

4. He is referring to women.

5. No. He believes that women have much more
power than the law says they do.

6. He believes women are more the masters than
the servants.

Making Connections

1. She uses words such as *tyrants* and *rebellion*,
knowing that these are reminders of colonial
objections toward the unfair use of power
exercised by Britain.

2. His response was very typical. He took it better
than most. That she felt comfortable bringing it
up says a lot about their relationship.

3. Women made bandages and provided
alternatives to boycotted tea and British
manufactured goods.

4. Women such as Abigail kept farms solvent
while husbands were away, working in ways
that they never had before.

Relating the Past to Our Lives

1. Answers will vary.

2. Answers will vary. Sample answer: Women have
equality in legal rights today. But for a number
of reasons, economic equality has not been
completely achieved.

3. Answers will vary. Sample answer: Today the
boundaries are quite blurred. Women's sports
exist, women have access to virtually any job,
and some men stay home while women work or
at least try to pitch in with housework. But the
gender difference in certain jobs such as politics
and business still exists, with the male-to-
female ratio in important posts
disproportionate.

Essay Topics

Essays will vary.

1. Essays may focus on what she would not have
wanted. For example, she did not want the
right to vote or to hold office. Abigail really

was concerned about the oppression of wives
and the idea of coverture, which means wives
have virtually no property or civil rights. In
many cases, husbands could physically abuse
their wives legally, although this did not
happen in her marriage.

2. Answers will vary.

3. Essays may include that owning property
establishes one's economic independence, can
provide for children as heirs, and, in colonial
society, was a requirement to vote.

The Declaration of Independence
Comprehension Questions

1. a) The colonies intend to separate from the
British Empire. b) The purpose is to explain the
reasons for this separation to the world.

2. They are born with the rights to life, liberty,
and the pursuit of happiness. Something self-
evident does not need to be proven.

3. Change the government or do away with it.

4. He sums it up as repeated abuse. He says the
king's intention is to establish a tyrannical
government.

5. Answers will vary.

6. They are referring to God.

7. Before God and the world, the representatives
of the people of the American colonies officially
declare our independence.

8. Their physical safety, their future, and all that
they stand for are at stake.

Critical Thinking

1. They are eliminating any connection with the
rights or responsibilities they had as British
citizens. It is too important a decision not to
explain it.

2. It exists to protect the natural rights of its
citizens. The power derives from the people.
"Consent of the governed" refers to the
agreement of the people to be ruled by their
government.

3. Answers will vary.

4. The parts are an introduction and statement of
purpose, supporting ideas, and a concluding
statement.

5. Answers will vary. Students may point out that
by signing the Declaration, each man legally

became a traitor to Britain and thus eligible for the death penalty.

Making Connections

1. Answers will vary. Sample answers: For such an important step, reasons need to be given.
2. The Coercive (or Intolerable) Acts—"For cutting off trade with all parts of the world"; "For taking away our charters, abolishing our most valuable laws, and altering fundamentally the forms of our governments"
   The Quartering Acts—"For quartering large bodies of armed troops among us"
   The Admiralty Courts for smuggling—"For depriving us in many cases, of the benefits of trial by jury"
   The Quebec Act—"For abolishing the free system of English laws in a neighboring province, establishing therein an arbitrary government, and enlarging its boundaries so as to render it at once an example and fit instrument for introducing the same absolute rule in these colonies"
   No taxation without representation—"For imposing taxes on us without our consent"
   The hiring of Hessians to fight in the war—"He is at this time transporting large armies of foreign mercenaries to complete the works of death, desolation and tyranny, already begun with circumstances of cruelty and perfidy scarcely paralleled in the most barbarous ages, and totally unworthy of the head of a civilized nation."
3. Answers will vary. Rights may include establishing diplomatic relations with other countries by exchanging ambassadors and respect for a nation's territorial boundaries.

Relating the Past to Our Lives

1–3. Answers will vary.

Essay Questions

Essays will vary.

1. Essays may include the status of women, African Americans, and Indians at the time of Jefferson's statement. Today much has been improved for those groups politically, but some economic disparities remain.
2. Essays may include being aware of contemporary events and voting in accordance

with one's beliefs. Today, the United States ranks among the lowest of world democracies in voter turnout, with barely more than half of eligible Americans voting in a presidential election.

3. Essays may include the idea of unanimity to show how sure the colonies were. A less than unanimous declaration might have been a problem depending on the size and location of the colonies objecting. For example, Massachusetts, New York, and Virginia were particularly important.
4. Essays may include that the natural rights cited and the concept of government agreed to by the people who are governed cut across all cultures and time periods. It is radical because it does not acknowledge traditional hierarchies; it states that basic rights are granted by God, not any ruler; and, particularly, it is an invitation for oppressed peoples to overthrow their rulers.

Slave Journey

Comprehension Questions

1. He saw a ship.
2. They were housed inside below the decks.
3. He first noticed the smell.
4. The heat and crowded conditions caused them to sweat.
5. The sweat and smells (he thought) led to disease.
6. He was depressed and upset, and he was very young.
7. They preferred death to the life they were enduring and would face.
8. Two drowned and one was saved.
9. It landed at Bridge Town, Barbados.
10. Merchants and planters boarded the ship.

Critical Thinking

1. He was from Africa's interior, so he had never seen a ship before.
2. He had no past experience with Europeans. He was imagining the worst.
3. They were containers that served as toilets.
4. The captives were worth money to the slavers, and they wanted to discourage any attempts to escape.
5. They were checking to make sure the Africans

were healthy.

Making Connections

1. It was a combination of climate and the labor intensity of sugar cane cultivation.
2. The price slaves sold for depended in part on a healthy appearance.
3. Check students' maps.

Relating the Past to Our Lives

1. Answers will vary.
2. Answers will vary. Sample answer: There are reports of slavery still in the Sudan and other parts of the world, although slavery is no longer legal anywhere; child prostitution and child labor also exist.
3. Answers will vary. Answers may include creativity, tenacity, flexibility, and strength of mind.

Essay Questions

Essays will vary.

1. Essays may include the issue of memory lapses and the tendency to interpret events with a broader context. The experiences also may be exaggerated to make a point.
2. Essays may include the fact that it was the date the French Revolution began. The American Revolution had already happened, Enlightenment ideas of natural rights were in the air, and many countries including England, France, and the United States were debating the morality of slavery at the time.
3. Essays may include that it might cause power vacuums filled by strong leaders who pledge to protect, it would destabilize parts of Africa, and it might cause ethnic conflict.

"What Is an American?"

Comprehension Questions

1. Missing are: great lords who own everything, aristocratic families, kings and their courts, religious institutions with great power and wealth, and great manufacturers.
2. They came mainly from Europe.
3. He describes a man who had an English grandfather, a Dutch wife, and four sons married to women of four different national origins.

4. The different way of life causes the changes.
5. They become "a new race of men."
6. Rewards come equivalent to the work.
7. A lord or abbot might claim it.
8. He must change his opinions and ideas from being a dependent to being rewarded by the fruits of his labor.

Critical Thinking

1. Class differences are not so great in America.
2. People can keep what they earn without "superiors" taking it from them; also implied is that America has a lot of land and resources.
3. Traditional hierarchies make it impossible for the poor to rise in status.
4. Answers will vary. Sample answer: In many ways it will depend on the stage of someone's life when arriving and the type of prejudice, but for many it may give a fresh perspective.
5. Answers will vary. Sample answer: America is unlike any nation that exists in the Old World because of the opportunities offered in a country just beginning and without set patterns.
6. Answers will vary. Sample answer: His impression may be too optimistic, since many people will struggle in the new country, but the difference in opportunity is real.

Making Connections

1. It is similar to the melting pot theory; Crèvecoeur even uses the word "melted" to describe the blending of a variety of backgrounds into a "new race of men." The only difference might be that by the twentieth century the concept of the American character was well established, which was not so in 1783.
2. Answers will vary. Sample answer: Crèvecoeur does not consider them to be among the future members of the new American system.
3. Answers will vary. Sample answer: Most of those who came to America did so with very little wealth, but the opportunities, especially in the form of the availability of land, made stark poverty less likely. It also takes a long time for disparities in wealth to develop.

Relating the Past to Our Lives

1. Answers will vary.
2. Answers will vary.

3. Answers will vary.
4. Many more today come from China, Korea, Japan, Cambodia, India, the Philippines, and Mexico.
5. Answers will vary.

Essay Questions

Essays will vary.

1. Essays may center on differences in pace of life, recreation, and how one makes a living. Sometimes how a person makes a living contributes to differences in political views. Red states and blue states may be explored for differences in region.
2. Essays may include the end of slavery and segregation and ongoing attempts at equity for African Americans, but continued disproportionate poverty. The mistreatment of Native Americans is acknowledged today, and political rights have been established. But poverty and unemployment on reservations are rife, especially where there are no gambling casinos to provide income.
3. Essays may include that immigrants today enter an already established society, with far greater wealth disparity, and due to immigration laws, many immigrants now arrive with skills and wealth. For those that enter poor, rising quickly in social class is more difficult, but not impossible. Similarities include the need to learn the language and the connection one feels to the country of origin.

George Washington's Farewell Address

Comprehension Questions

1. The American public is the audience.
2. The election is for the U.S. presidency.
3. He will not be a candidate.
4. Political parties distract legislative bodies, weaken government, excite the public with jealousy and hatred, even start riots and rebellions, and allow for foreign involvement.
5. It is good to extend trade relations.
6. Permanent political alliances should be avoided.
7. Alliances that had been made previous to his address need to be honored.

Critical Thinking

1. They both can excite the public and create opportunities for corruption.
2. Answers will vary. Sample answer: No. He fears military alliances above all. Trade relations do not bother him.
3. Answers will vary. Sample answer: Perhaps it was for him because Washington felt the direction of the country threatened its future, and he felt it was his responsibility to address this.
4. Answers will vary. Sample answer: Perhaps some felt less comfortable. But many were caught up in the partisan warfare, and they probably saw the defeat of their opponents as the only insurance for a future.

Making Connections

1. He is referring to the idea that the Republican Party had a firm foundation in the South, while the Federalists were strong in the North. The parties were sectional.
2. Given what Washington warned against, he would oppose both.
3. He set a precedent that later presidents followed.
4. Answers may include the rise of political parties, friction with France and England, Jay's Treaty, the Whiskey Rebellion, and the Citizen Genet affair, among others.

Relating the Past to Our Lives

1. Answers will vary.
2. Answers will vary. Sample answer: He would call a press conference that would be televised.
3. Answers will vary.

Essay Questions

Essays will vary.

1. Essays may include how political parties and foreign alliances have become far more of a factor than Washington could have imagined, but he also could not predict the realities of the modern world's weapons, communications, economic, and transportation systems.
2. Essays may include that with his advice, given the modern world's weapons, communications, economic, and transportation systems, the United States could not stay safely in isolation. The country would eventually be drawn in to

world involvement.

3. Essays may include that parties help get out the vote, recruit candidates, raise issues, and organize Congress, among other things.

The Louisiana Purchase

Comprehension Questions

1. It is a letter, addressed to Robert Livingston (U.S. minister to France).
2. France has acquired Louisiana and Florida from Spain.
3. France was a natural friend.
4. Its ownership of New Orleans now makes it a natural enemy.
5. Spain is weak and interested in peace.
6. France is much more powerful and aggressive.
7. The United States must become friends with Britain and build up its own navy.
8. He hopes France will be willing to give up New Orleans.

Critical Thinking

1. The main idea is that France's possession of Louisiana puts American commerce at risk, so some effort must be made to convince France to sell New Orleans and some of Florida.
2. He said that the United States could never continue as friends with France as long it was in control of New Orleans.
3. It is a snap judgment based on recent dealings with both countries. Napoleon's rule was far different from that of his predecessors.
4. Parts of the letter include that before this acquisition, France has been a "natural friend" of the United States with many common interests, that any nation owning New Orleans immediately becomes an enemy, that French control of New Orleans means the possibility of a U.S. alliance with England, and that selling New Orleans to the United States can make France a friend again.

Making Connections

1. France had supported the Americans in their revolution against Britain.
2. Answers will vary. Sample answer: Perhaps future conflict would result when settlers moved west later in the century.

3. It meant that settlers would be coming into their land and pushing them off it. It meant the end to their way of life.
4. What made America so full of opportunity was the availability of land; with it there was always a chance to start over.

Relating the Past to Our Lives

1. The states include all or most parts of thirteen states: Louisiana, Arkansas, Missouri, Iowa, Minnesota, North Dakota, South Dakota, Nebraska, Oklahoma, Kansas, Montana, Wyoming, and Colorado.
2. Answers will vary. Sample answer: Communication is faster, and diplomatic talks are heavily covered by the media.
3. Answers will vary.

Essay Questions

Essays will vary.

1. Essays may include the positive outcomes of room to grow and remain agrarian, the resources it brought, and removal of a foreign country west of the Mississippi River. Negatives may include conflict with Native Americans, and eventual conflict with Mexico.
2. Essays may include that Jefferson saw a deal that he could not pass up. He also believed deeply that the country must remain a nation of yeoman farmers. The land allowed for that far into the future.
3. Essays may include that he probably was not bluffing. As much as he preferred France over England, he knew the importance of New Orleans to American farmers and the nation's economy. Jefferson was a pragmatist, as the purchase shows.

The Monroe Doctrine

Comprehension Questions

1. He warns them not to try to make new colonies in the Western Hemisphere.
2. The United States has stayed out of wars that do not involve it.
3. The United States would defend itself if it were threatened.
4. It is most connected to its own hemisphere—the Western.

5. European nations' political system is quite different.
6. The United States considers any European involvement in the Western Hemisphere as a threat.
7. The United States will not interfere with existing European colonies.
8. Monroe warns against taking the new nations as colonies or interfering with their political systems.
9. The United States will continue to stay out of Europe's affairs.

Critical Thinking

1. Answers will vary. Sample answer: To ask a nation to give up long-standing colonies would be asking more than a European country would be willing to accept, so insisting on this might require U.S. intervention. The United States was in no position to go to war. Intervening in existing colonies would also involve interfering in the affairs of other governments.
2. He means that European countries are governed mostly as monarchies.
3. Just as the United States has stayed out of European affairs, the United States is asking Europe to stay out of American affairs.
4. The United States realized that, due to economic interests, England would back the United States.
5. Not interfering in the affairs of European countries was something the United States always practiced. Any new involvement by Europe in the hemisphere could not avoid "endangering our peace and happiness." Thus to stay out would be an even trade of remaining uninvolved in each other's business.

Making Connections

1. Since they were not consulted on the Doctrine, some probably felt the United Sates was involving itself in their future without being asked to do so. Others may have felt grateful that they would not have to worry about fighting European nations to remain independent.
2. It fears Old World influence—its governments, and social structure. To keep the Old from infecting the New, the United States sought to remove European influence as much as possible.

3. It is not isolation because commercial and diplomatic relations would still exist. It is more of a "spheres of influence" philosophy. Leading countries have their neighborhoods and will keep the peace in those neighborhoods.
4. While today the State of the Union is televised and reporters hang on every word, annual messages then were for congressional consumption. They were written messages to be read by Congress. These annual messages were considered important and would be read by most members of Congress, so including the Monroe Doctrine in his annual message was a good strategy for Monroe. Also, European publications would probably carry reports about the annual message, which would spread the message of the Monroe Doctrine to European governments and politicians.

Relating the Past to Our Lives

1. Answers will vary.
2. Answers will vary.
3. Answers will vary. Sample Answer: George W. Bush's policy of preemptive attack of countries that threaten the United States.

Essay Questions

Essays will vary.
1. Essays may include as similarities that in both cases Europe was the concern and that both dealt with foreign entanglements. A difference was that the Monroe Doctrine actually was an entanglement itself because it committed the United States to action against a European nation that interfered in the hemisphere. It promotes foreign involvement, which Washington's address warned against.
2. Essays may include that with nuclear weapons and terrorists, the doctrine has become less relevant. It matters less now that the United States has enemies physically close.
3. Essays may include that with nuclear weapons and terrorists today, how close a foreign presence is to our borders becomes less a concern. Globalism renders the Monroe Doctrine less relevant.

The Liberator

Comprehension Questions

1. It is written to the public.
2. The subject is the abolition of slavery.
3. He felt that the North was most sympathetic.
4. He found the most opposition in the South.
5. He cites the Declaration of Independence.
6. It must end immediately.
7. He apologizes for arguing for gradual abolition earlier in his life.
8. He declares he will not compromise or give up.

Critical Thinking

1. Garrison wanted to make the purpose of the newspaper clear at the outset.
2. He is comparing the newspaper to a battleship with its flag flying.
3. Certain problems need to be solved immediately because they are emergencies. Opinions about Garrison's comparisons will vary.
4. They summarize Garrison's reasoning that slavery must end immediately, and they are dramatic.
5. His tone of voice would be loud.

Making Connections

Answers will vary. Sample answers:

1. He is saying that all men are brothers because they are human.
2. He uses the words because it is the formative statement of our national ideals.
3. He was particularly blunt in his description of racist Northerners. The tone works because his message that slavery is an emergency comes through when it seems that the writer shows emotion. He wants to get people's attention.
4. The civil rights movement of the 1950s and 1960s and the antiwar movement of the 1960s and 1970s have stirred similar emotions.
5. Slavery was growing despite those methods.
6. The obstacles included the following: fear that the South would leave the Union; the economic effect on the South which would affect Northern manufacturers.

Relating the Past to Our Lives

1. Answers will vary.
2. Answers will vary. Sample answer: There has not been much on the national level today, although the Iraq war stirred some emotions. Globally, the World Trade Organization meetings have caused violent protests.
3. Answers will vary. Sample answer: Some people find compromising necessary in politics, but they are unwilling to compromise on moral issues.
4. Answers will vary.

Essay Questions

Essays will vary.

1. Essays may include that it was clear that a gradualist approach would take many years if it worked at all; that Garrison and those like him forced the issue into the public eye; that Garrison and others contributed to a polarizing of viewpoints in the country, which eventually led to the war.
2. Essays may include gradualist approaches such as running antislavery political candidates who pledge to end slavery. Advantage: It would be trying to solve the problem within the system. Disadvantage: It would take a long to time to get a majority, if one could ever be reached.
3. If students agree, essays may include that they forced the issue, never letting it leave the public eye and making it a question of morality. If students disagree, essays may include that what actually raised the slavery question constantly was the addition of western territories, creating crises.

The Trail of Tears

Comprehension Questions

1. He is the chief.
2. The intended audience is the United States Congress.
3. They sent a group to Washington in 1835 to work out the disagreement.
4. A small group of individual Cherokee made a treaty, called the Treaty of New Echota.
5. They did not represent the Cherokee nation; they had no legal status.
6. The Senate approved the treaty by one vote.
7. Their land, their property, and their humanity have been taken away.
8. The Cherokee are overwhelmed and heartsick.
9. The treaty is unjust and cannot be enforced by

a fair people.

10. He asks Congress not to enforce the treaty.

Critical Thinking

1. "And we are constrained solemnly to declare, that we cannot but contemplate the enforcement of the stipulations of this instrument on us, against our consent, as an act of injustice and oppression, which, we are well persuaded, can never knowingly be countenanced by the Government and people of the United States; nor can we believe it to be the design of these honorable and highminded individuals, who stand at the head of the Govt., to bind a whole Nation, by the acts of a few unauthorized individuals."

2. Ross is accurate. Senators probably knew that, since it was not unusual to get unpopular treaties officially accepted by Indian tribes in that manner.

3. Although the Cherokee have a few allies in the Senate, the public is not clamoring for justice. Without that, the Senate will not satisfy his request.

4. The tone is respectful and pleading, somewhat desperate in places.

5. He did what American citizens would do. While not citizens, the Cherokee believed in the U.S. system of government and adopted a similar one.

Making Connections

1. Answers will vary. Sample answer: settlers entering their land, the state of Georgia ordering their removal and enforcing Georgia law within tribal areas.

2. The U.S. government wants the land open for settlement by whites. In the Cherokee case, gold was found on their land.

3. It is 800 miles. At 2 miles per hour, it would take 400 hours.

Relating the Past to Our Lives

1. Answers will vary.

2. Answers will vary. Sample answer: One event was the ethnic cleansing in the former Yugoslavia. The Cherokee removal was ethnic cleansing.

3. Answers will vary. Sample answer: No. Today minority rights are much more protected. Any

U.S. president today would feel obligated to enforce a Supreme Court decision.

Essay Questions

Essays will vary.

1. Essays may include that it shows how important the land was to the tribe and that the Cherokee understood that the government might use a "divide and conquer" approach. Some may not consider it a capital crime today.

2. Essays may include that Jackson felt that they would be in constant conflict with whites. However, they were moved to a land that was not economically suited to their way of life.

3. Essays may include that it was a good decision because they did not abandon their principles, or that it was a bad decision because they did not get what they wanted or the money that might have made life easier in Oklahoma.

The Lowell Mills

Comprehension Questions

1. She plans to quit her job.

2. She urges Ellen to stay.

3. She dislikes getting up early, the noise of the mills, and the length of the workday.

4. She agrees that these conditions are not fun, and she points out that all jobs have disadvantages.

5. The workers have unsupervised free time in the evenings when they can attend activities to improve their minds.

6. She says that those activities cost money and could leave a worker broke, far from family.

7. She says there are few social class differences, and a person only has to have good character to have friends.

8. There is not enough time to eat, drink, or sleep; life is regulated by a bell; the workers are treated like machines.

9. Even on a farm a person is woken up by noise.

10. The silence of the farm can be dull.

11. They finally agreed that even with its disadvantages, a factory job is the best.

12. Answers will vary.

Critical Thinking

Answers will vary. Sample answers:

1. Any disadvantage that would endanger health should be more important than having to get up early.

2. It is a subject very relevant to the writer's audience—the other girls.

3. The dialogue encapsulates the advantages and disadvantages of Lowell. If girls were not having similar discussions, then they were probably having an internal dialogue along similar lines.

4. In the early part of Lowell's history, working conditions were better. At that point, the trade-off made more sense.

5. They may be happy with it to some extent, since it attempts to be balanced. But they would probably prefer something less balanced and more in their favor.

Making Connections

Answers will vary. Sample answers:

1. Yes. People often write fiction based on their experiences.

2. It is livelier to read a dialogue than an essay discussing the issues. The factory girls could relate to it. The author may even have taken part in a similar conversation.

3. No. They believed working at Lowell to be a short-time event to help with family finances or spend some time on their own. Marriage was the goal for most. During this era women rarely worked at a paying job once married.

4. Women and textiles were a natural combination, as women carded and spun at home. Otherwise, it did not fit. Therefore the mill owners included lectures, dorms, church, and other elements to more closely conform to societal expectations.

Relating the Past to Our Lives

1–3. Answers will vary.

Essay Questions

Essays will vary.

1. Answers will vary.

2. Essays may include that young women were able to participate in the wider world, have some control over their personal economy, and attend events that were probably unavailable at

home. At the same time, women were exploited with lower wages and an increasing workload.

3. Essays may include that these interests were not mutually exclusive—to some extent, looking out for the young women's welfare, at least at first, helped recruit and keep a low-paid work-force. But as the later history of the mills shows, when forced to make a choice, the owners chose profit over workers' welfare.

Conditions for the Mentally Ill

Comprehension Questions

1. Her audience is the Massachusetts legislature.

2. She visited prisons and almshouses in towns near Boston.

3. She found criminals, paupers, "idiots," and "insane persons."

4. It is revolting, especially to women, but the truth must be told.

5. She found them in cages, closets, cellars, stalls, and pens.

6. The lawmakers are to blame.

7. Students should list three of these towns: Lincoln, Medford, Pepperell, Brookfield, Granville, Dedham.

8. She asks them to defend those that are helpless.

9. Convicts are also suffering.

Critical Thinking

1. Massachusetts mistreats mentally challenged and insane people by housing them with criminals and poor people.

2. She speaks from direct observation using specific details to illustrate.

3. A successful result would be to house mentally ill people in a separate facility where the staff would try to cure them.

4. She organizes it as an essay with an introduction, evidence, and a conclusion.

5. Yes. The Massachusetts legislature had the power to change the way the state treated mentally ill people.

Making Connections

1. Legislators who had a part in the "defective legislation" Dix refers to as the reason for the problem would take offense.

2. They were being housed in that way because

they were misunderstood. It was convenient to put them out of sight, and no one before then spoke for them.

3. Women were considered to be responsible for the moral aspects of the home. This was extended to the moral aspects of society.

4. They were shut away where no one could see them.

5. She could see the possibility of people being able to change and to learn.

6. As a general rule, women did not speak in public, especially to men.

Relating the Past to Our Lives

1. Answers will vary.
2. Answers will vary.
3. Answers will vary. Sample answer: Today patients receive medication, or therapy, or a combination of the two. Hospitalization is less common.

Essay Questions

Essays will vary.

1. Essays may include that it was the age of equality of the common person, one that sought improvements in society. Reformers thought people could change if given the means.

2. Essays may include that the message was similar in that each writer believed change was needed immediately. The audience is clearly different. Garrison's tone was much more strident.

3. Essays might include that many reformers are religiously inspired and believe in the perfectability of people. Many reforms fit within a similar approach to society's problems.

The Mexican War

Comprehension Questions

1. The U.S. Congress was the audience.
2. Polk sent a representative to speak with the Mexican government and resolve all differences.
3. The Mexican government refused to see the envoy.
4. Mexico invaded U.S. territory and killed Americans.
5. He had placed troops between the Nueces and Rio Grande (del Norte).
6. It threatened to invade due to Texas joining the

United States.

7. It claimed the Rio Grande (del Norte) as the southern boundary.
8. The Mexican army attacked the American troops.
9. Sixteen were killed and wounded.
10. Mexico was entirely at fault, according to Polk.

Critical Thinking

1. He wants Congress to understand that he has tried to avoid war.
2. He favors this boundary because he posted troops between the Nueces and the del Norte (Rio Grande), and this boundary gives Texas more territory.
3. With the boundary at the Nueces in Mexican minds, American troops are in Mexican territory.
4. According to Polk, the U.S. government played no part in starting the war. This is not entirely accurate. Both the U.S. annexation of Texas and sending U.S. troops into the disputed territory between the Nueces and the del Norte were clear provocations, as was Frémont's military expedition into Mexico's California territory.
5. A war declaration will not approach the issues evenhandedly, because the president is trying to persuade Congress to accept war.
6. The reasons include Mexico's refusal to meet with the U.S. envoy and Mexican troops crossing into the territory north of the Rio del Norte and firing on U.S. troops there. The military action is the most serious problem. The attempt to reopen diplomatic relations is potentially the easiest to settle in a friendly way.

Making Connections

1. He is in effect asking for war, though he says a state of war already exists. Under the U.S. Constitution, Congress declares war.
2. The Mexican government suspected that the U.S. government was behind the Texas independence movement.
3. Many thought it was a war waged to extend slavery; others thought justification for the war was inadequate.
4. Check students' maps.
5. The War of 1812, the Vietnam War, and the war in Iraq are among the most controversial in

addition to the Mexican War.

Relating the Past to Our Lives

1. Students may take either position. A *yes* may include that U.S. soldiers had been killed, an interest in acquiring more land, and manifest destiny. A *no* may include that the reasons for war were contrived by the administration, which did not want to raise the slavery issue.
2. They probably see it as the United States picking a fight to take land.
3. There is more economic opportunity.

Essay Questions

Essays will vary.

1. Essays may include these factors: U.S. aggression, those who believed in manifest destiny, slaveholders, and Mexican President Santa Anna.
2. Essays may include that if by "United States" the question refers to the Polk administration, the answer is yes. Expansion of boundaries and acquisition of the Southwest was a goal—with or without war. Polk was left with only the war option at that point.
3. Essays may include for short-term influences that the acquisition opened the slavery question again, leading to the Compromise of 1850; also, the gold rush in 1849 was on land formerly owned by Mexico. Long-term influences may include mineral wealth and illegal Mexican immigrants populating the region.

The California Gold Rush

Comprehension Questions

1. He wanted to go right away to the gold rush in California.
2. Luzena insisted on coming with him.
3. They would make their fortune.
4. They brought a bed, food (bacon, flour), pots, kettles, and a cow.
5. They left at sunrise.
6. It was ferried across.
7. She was terrified of Indians (at first), because of the stories she had read and heard about attacks on other settlers.
8. They were friendly and traded goods with the wagon train.
9. Their train had six wagons. Wagon trains preceded and trailed theirs as far as the eye could see.
10. She complains about the plodding and unvarying monotony, the emotional highs and lows, the weary repetition of routine, the meager food, and of being tired, dusty, ill-tempered, and worn out of patience.
11. They put the wagon bed up on blocks to raise it above water level.
12. The wagon and its oxen were pulled under by quicksand and disappeared.

Critical Thinking

1. According to her, that because they had so little, they had nothing to lose. But her mention of Indians reminds the reader that the Wilsons could have lost their lives.
2. It was hard to predict the difficulties on the trail until one was on it. Less weight became more important than keeping certain items.
3. She thought it was both boring and frightening.
4. They could help one another, share knowledge and materials, and band together if attacked.
5. Writing it after having survived the journey would not be as desperate as a journal kept by someone wondering if he or she will survive.
6. She writes as if it is a great adventure, although boring at times. But as mentioned above, that may not have been the way she felt at the time.
7. Day-to-day fears and monotony might be expressed in a more emotional way.

Making Connections

1. Physical features include the Rocky Mountains and a great stretch of prairie and desert with unknown quantities of water.
2. It is approximately 2,000 miles.
3. It was reasonable in that some wagon trains were attacked. To consider all Indians unfriendly would be unfair, but natural. Many Native Americans understood what the westward movement meant for them.
4. Women often did things along the trail that they would not do at home. For example, they drove ox teams and collected buffalo chips (dung) for fuel.

Relating the Past to Our Lives

1. Answers will vary.

2. Answers will vary. Sample answer: For many, the entertainment industry attracts. For others, it is the climate.
3. Answers will vary.

Essay Questions

Essays will vary.

1. Answers will vary.
2. Essays may include the people looking for a fresh start, free land, and finding the area one lived in too "crowded."
3. Essays may include inner strength, ability to work together, creativity, and courage.

Women's Rights

Comprehension Questions

1. She is kept out of the religious ministry; she is made to follow laws enacted for her by men; she must promise to obey her husband and admit inferiority.
2. She compares this with women's status in Asian countries.
3. It has hurt them.
4. Their rights disappear.
5. Legal reforms are needed.
6. The husband can take his wife's wages as his.
7. She wants removal of obstacles to women's rise in status and encouragement to do so.

Critical Thinking

1. Answers will vary. Sample answer: She makes her points by always supporting claims with specific evidence.
2. Mott's intended audience is men.
3. Mott's purpose is to try to convince readers of injustice done to women.
4. Women have been successfully taught to like their subservient positions.
5. It is 1849, and slavery is the issue of the day. The audience might very well have been people sympathetic to abolitionism.

Making Connections

1. Men need to take action, because by law, they hold office and make laws.
2. Only women in poor families needed to work for wages.
3. Quakers had advanced ideas on women's rights. Women could speak at meetings and travel

alone.
4. Most, even those sympathetic to other reforms, would reject the ideas. Her ideas were far in advance of even the most liberal men (and most women).
5. They grew up in a society that subordinated women. They learned and believed it was normal.

Relating the Past to Our Lives

1. Answers will vary.
2. Answers will vary. Sample answer: Equal protection laws have made legal equality a reality. There remain inequalities at the workplace in that women are not as well represented in certain types of jobs, and they may be paid less for doing the same work as men.
3. Answers will vary.

Essay Questions

Essays will vary.

1. Essays may include that people, especially women, who worked in the abolitionist movement noticed that the rights they championed for black slaves—such as the right to direct their own lives as they saw fit and the right to vote—were denied to women.
2. Essays may select the removal of the law of coverture. If women were in abusive relationships, they had no recourse.
3. Essays may include that it was originally a lecture she gave in response to a man's speech denying that women should have more rights. The tone seems to express the effect of observing an accumulation of injustices over time.

The Compromise of 1850

Comprehension Questions

1. Henry Clay proposed them.
2. The purpose was to settle the questions surrounding slavery among the states and return the country to harmony.
3. The resolution proposes that Congress do nothing regarding slavery in California. (*Note:* California had asked to be admitted as a free state. Congress taking no position allows

California to get what it asked.)

4. The territorial governments will not take a stand on slavery.
5. It deals with the boundary of Texas.
6. The United States will pay for Texas's public debt in exchange for the state giving up any claim to territory in New Mexico.
7. It gives these reasons: the existence of slavery in Maryland; the lack of choice among Washington, D.C., residents; and the lack of compensation offered to slaveholders.
8. The selling of slaves within Washington, D.C., will be prohibited.
9. A law should be passed to more effectively return runaways who were "bound to service." (*Note:* This means slaves.)
10. Slavery will still exist.

Critical Thinking

1. California will be admitted as a free state.
2. It will be left to the people of the state when they create a state constitution.
3. Conducting slave auctions in plain view bothered many legislators, and it also embarrassed them when viewed by foreign visitors. Also, some Northerners thought that eliminating this trade was a beginning of perhaps nibbling away at slavery.
4. It refers to slaves.
5. Slave states: the stronger Fugitive Slave Law and preserving slavery in D.C. Free states: California admitted as a free state and abolishing the slave trade in D.C.

Making Connections

1. Compromises include the Great Compromise during the Constitutional Convention and the Missouri Compromise.
2. Arkansas, Michigan, Florida, Texas, Iowa, Wisconsin
3. The South had a more rigid, hierarchical social structure; the Southern economy was based on cotton, while the Northern economy was based on industry; Southern wealth was measured more in land, while Northern wealth was measured more in capital.
4. The Compromise only dealt with the Louisiana Territory.
5. California as a free state tipped the balance so that more free states now existed; others may

have opposed slavery but not at the expense of the Union.
6. Article Four of the U.S. Constitution grants the federal government the right to make law in the territories. Most people at the time believed that Congress had no such right in the states.

Relating the Past to Our Lives

1. Answers will vary.
2. Answers will vary.
3. Answers will vary. Sample answers: The two houses of Congress regularly compromise about the different versions of a bill passed in each respective house to create one bill. This happened with the Bush tax cuts.

Essay Questions

Essays will vary.

1. Essays may include that compromises did not solve the basic problem; its solution was just postponed, leaving it festering.
2. Essays may include that sometimes compromise postpones a solution; sometimes a bold step would be preferable; compromises sometimes give the impression of no movement toward a solution.
3. Essays may include a constitutional amendment protecting slavery where it already existed or continuing the Missouri Compromise line to the Pacific Ocean.
4. Essays may include that the two compromises are similar in that they postpone the slavery question and require both sides to sacrifice. They are different in that since each part of the 1850 compromise had to be passed separately, only 21 percent of Congress voted for all parts. A majority passed the Missouri Compromise as one large bill.

"The Nature of Slavery"

Comprehension Questions

1. He was a slave for twenty years.
2. Both law and Southern religion sanction slavery.
3. The master has absolute power.
4. A slave has nothing under U.S. law.
5. He reminds the audience that a slave has a soul, hopes, emotions, and religious understanding.
6. The first job of a slave owner is to destroy the

things in a slave that make him or her a person.

7. The slave owner is reducing the slave to a machine.

8. They think of education as something that will undercut the slave system.

9. The nation cannot be at peace because of the guilt it has over slavery's existence.

Critical Thinking

1. The slave is property, like a horse or a cow.

2. Answers will vary. Sample answer: It tries to take away the slave's human qualities.

3. Answers will vary. Sample answer: Douglass functions as a primary source, bearing witness rather than speaking from secondhand sources, as most abolitionists had to do.

4. Answers will vary. Sample answer: It tapped his imagination, taking him away from slavery for that time, opening up possibilities, and letting him see the power of the mind.

5. Answers will vary. Sample answer: The slavery question will continue to fester under the surface because there is no compromise position.

6. Answers will vary. Sample answer: He begins by establishing credibility by citing his years in slavery. Throughout, he draws on his experience to illustrate his claims.

Making Connections

Answers will vary. Sample answers:

1. It puts the slaveholder in the position of oppressor, causing him to do things he otherwise would not do.

2. People were very religious at the time. Douglass believed that some churches aided and abetted slavery, which he saw as hypocrisy. He wanted to appeal to the true religion.

3. He was intelligent, articulate, uncompromising, and bold.

Relating the Past to Our Lives

1. Answers will vary. Sample answer: Douglass was also concerned with inequalities in Northern cities. He is likely to have been unhappy with the proportion of African Americans living in poverty. But he would have been pleased with the progress that has been made since he died, including the dismantling of Jim Crow.

2. Answers will vary. Sample answer: Bono of U2 has used his celebrity status to get access to world leaders to speak for canceling the debt of third world countries and getting AIDS drugs to Africa. He also has spoken on issues at universities.

3. Answers will vary.

Essay Questions

Essays will vary.

1. Essays may include that learning builds one's confidence, takes people places in their imagination, makes them aware of possibilities, teaches them to think for themselves, and opens them up to new ideas. This was more true than when other media did not exist.

2. Essays may include that both experiences were dehumanizing and unjust. Differences: Douglass was born into slavery and was always a part of it. He did not wonder what was happening and did not fear for his life as Olaudah Equiano did.

3. Essays may include that no compromise position can exist on the morality of slavery; as long as slavery existed, some people would agitate against it, causing tension; any political settlement ignores the human element.

The Gettysburg Address

Comprehension Questions

1. Four score and seven is eighty-seven. Lincoln is referring to 1776.

2. The United States was dedicated to establishing liberty and equality.

3. The war is testing whether a country based on those principles can survive.

4. The event is being held to dedicate the cemetery.

5. Their deaths have made it sacred.

6. No, he does not.

7. The world will remember what the soldiers did in the battle.

8. They should achieve what the soldiers died for.

Critical Thinking

1. He was referring to the founders of the country.

2. It is the founding document of the nation, and one that expresses national ideals regarding equality.

3. Lincoln does this because the Declaration says that all men are created equal.
4. As the nation begins again as a union, African-American former slaves will now be included among free people.
5. He was very precise and concise.

Making Connections

1. The words come from the Declaration of Independence.
2. It appeared that the North now had the upper hand and would eventually win.
3. He never believed the Southern states could leave the Union legally—therefore, they did not. For Lincoln, all participants in the battle were countrymen.

Relating the Past to Our Lives

1–3. Answers will vary.

Essay Questions

Essays will vary.
1. Essays may take issue with what the Declaration in fact meant by "all men are created equal"; the new birth of freedom will be a free Confederate nation; the response would agree with the importance of the sacrifice, but for a different cause.
2. Essays may include factors such as its timing, its brevity so people can read the whole thing, its eloquence, and its meaning.
3. Essays may include that we still need to live up to it, and that Lincoln was right in that it began a new era.
4. Essays may include that equality was not part of the Constitution, which sanctioned slavery; the Declaration was a more idealistic document; the later amendments try to add human equality to the Constitution.

The Reconstruction Amendments

Comprehension Questions

1. The Thirteenth Amendment bans slavery.
2. A person can be born a citizen or can become one through the process stated by law.
3. It is intended to limit the states' powers.
4. The states are prohibited from depriving a citizen of legal rights and equal treatment under the law.

5. Race, ethnic group, or whether the individual had been a slave cannot be considered.

Critical Thinking

1. The document consists of amendments to the U.S. Constitution.
2. They were written to prevent state governments from taking black rights away.
3. Each confers a higher level of rights.
4. Rights include the following: right to a lawyer, to a jury of your peers, to not incriminate yourself, to face your accusers in open court.

Making Connections

1. The Emancipation Proclamation only freed slaves in states in rebellion. All other slaves were not included.
2. They did not have many rights before passage of these amendments.
3. Such requirements as literacy tests and poll taxes are omitted.
4. The Southern states accepted the Thirteenth Amendment.
5. No. Otherwise, the Fifteenth Amendment would not have been needed. Women would have been able to vote also.

Relating the Past to Our Lives

1. Answers will vary.
2. Answers will vary.
3. Answers will vary. Sample answer: It deals with the equal protection of all citizens, a very hot topic over the years. Also, the Supreme Court has used the Fourteenth Amendment to incorporate or make much of the Bill of Rights apply to state law. That means that whenever a state law is reviewed by the Supreme Court, the Fourteenth Amendment is listed among the justifications.

Essay Questions

Essays will vary.
1. Essays may include that the end of slavery, citizenship for African Americans, and the right of black males begin a new era of justice for a group long oppressed; that the amendments attempt to have the nation live up to the Declaration of Independence.
2. Essays may include that for the Fourteenth Amendment, later court interpretation over what equality meant led to unintended

inequality not expected at the time the amendment was ratified; that Southern states passed laws that limited the right of black males to vote that did not violate the Fifteenth Amendment but did violate its intent; that most importantly, the American public seemed to lose interest in securing rights for African Americans in the South.

3. Essays may include that many women were outraged; some even made racist statements; others understood the practicality of trying to pass the vote for black men first.

4. Essays may include that racism is a state of mind, and changes of states of mind cannot be legislated; that traditional patterns are difficult to change.